ADVANCE PRAISE FOR *STA*

"As a TEDx organizer, I'm focused on the result of our speakers' efforts: The Talk. But in this book, I could instead focus on Chloe's experience as she traveled toward the red circle. Her gift for expressing deep thoughts helped bring those weeks to life for me, and her struggles with insecurities and doubts put a lens on the challenges she faced before taking that first step onto the stage. Rarely do we meet people who are gifted communicators, both in creating well-crafted stories and possessing the poise necessary to present them in a high stakes setting. Chloe's insight into the turmoil within a teenager's psyche is immensely readable."

MARK SYLVESTER, executive producer, TEDxSantaBarbara

"Chloe Howard is a true world changer. There is nothing more inspiring than someone who harnesses a painful experience for good. And there is no better example of that transformational spirit than Chloe. Being lucky enough to witness Chloe's meeting with Bono and see the incredible good she's done with that inspiration since inspires me to be braver in fighting for good, and I believe *Stand Beautiful* will do that for you as well."

MATTHEW POHLSON, cofounder, Omaze

"Chloe's story [*Stand Beautiful*] is a contemporary, vulnerable account of personal experience, empathy, and evangelism that serves as an inspiring reminder that we are all unique, broken, and imperfect; yet God unconditionally sees us, accepts us, and loves us. It's a *beautiful* testimony of trust, transformation, and triumph—in Jesus.

BRIAN M. VAN HALL, FACHE COO, CURE International

"Wow. I'm impressed. And I don't say this lightly. Chloe's book is incredible. The strength this seventeen-year-old shares while in the midst of bullying is appropriate not only for teens but for adults who experience tough battles in life. We all get knocked down, but Chloe's resolve, tenacity, and solidity through the worst times in her life are an encouragement to all of us! Again: WOW."

DR. SUSIE SHELLENBERGER, speaker and writer

"Like Emily Doe, Chloe Howard transformed her victimhood into a superpower. These remarkable young women share the gift of inspiration. Being the victim of a crime can make you feel mute and powerless. But Chloe uses her strength, her spirituality, and her clear, powerful voice to call out to those who have suffered bullying. Chloe's ode to finding self-worth is an important message for anyone who has felt the sting of self-doubt or the humiliation of harassment: Stand Beautiful."

JEFF ROSEN, Santa Clara County District Attorney

"Oftentimes victims suffer in silence, but not Chloe. She's fighting back with a verbal punch to get the justice she deserves. In standing up for herself, she's standing for all young people who have been bullied and assaulted. Her voice is powerful, and she is courageous and fierce. She's truly a role model for young women, and this book should be required reading in all high schools."

ALALEH KIANERCI, Santa Clara County Prosecutor
of the Brock Turner Stanford sexual assault case

"I've been working with teenagers for more than thirty-five years; and while there are many reasons I continue, one of my top reasons is how hopeful I continue to find them to be. Reading a story like Chloe's could be discouraging if you focus on the problems it reveals. But, ultimately, it's a story of overcoming, a story of redemption, a story of passion to change the world and we all need more of that ... I know I do."

Doug Fields, founder of Download Youth Ministry
and author of *Purpose Driven Youth Ministry*

"Chloe's powerful reflection of her abuse at the hands of young bullies and the lessons she has learned on her journey make *Stand Beautiful* a gift of hope to anyone who has faced humiliation and wondered if any good could ever come from it. It's a gripping story with a strong message for anyone who wants to rise above the spirit of darkness in our world today and bring hope that we can do better."

Mark Matlock, president of WisdomWorks and author of
Faith for Exiles and *Living a Life That Matters*

"Think of a quilt, a homemade-with-love-kind of blanket with all the different squares. Got it? Now, on those squares, write the repeated words *provision, protection, meaning,* and *belonging.* These are the four basic desires of us, as humans, that are all woven together like a quilt in this quest for our humanity. The squares of us intertwine to create a beautiful picture through us, but only one square at a time. However, every once in a while, I hear a story, meet a human, that brings us beyond our own pictures and lets us look upon the whole tapestry that is humanity at one time. Chloe's story will cover you with the common threads of humanity, give you a bigger picture of your own story, and challenge you to stand beautiful in your own square of this beautiful thing called life. This is not a book, but a vision."

Eric Samuel Timm, orator, artist, and author of
Static Jedi: The Art of Hearing God Through the Noise

"*Stand Beautiful* is a powerful and meaningful book that needs to be read, understood, and appreciated. The author, although young, has much to say, and there is much to be learned from her writing. I teach a class in Disabilities, and this is the kind of text that can be used to help students, as well as others, navigate the importance and complexities that surround this subject."

JEFF BANKS, Ph.D., Professor of Teaching of Humanities
and Teacher Education at Pepperdine University

"Mark Twain once said, 'The two most important days of your life are the day you were born and the day you discover why.' Chloe has written a beautiful account of the way in which her own experience of human suffering arising from a birth defect helped her discover God's greater purpose for her life. Her sensitive, articulate account demonstrates that there is nothing predictable in this process. In fact, Chloe's amazing story unveils her own discovery of why her life was created, how she is fearfully and wonderfully made, and what her life contribution will ultimately include. This book is sure to bring hope and comfort to countless millions who must pivot away from the crucibles of suffering at the hands of other humans to find God's greater purposes for their life. Chloe's narrative is sure to inspire a positive, hopeful engagement with all that life brings."

GAYLE D. BEEBE, PhD, president of Westmont College

"In a world that tends to whisper you're 'never enough,' there is a need for voices and stories that affirm that we really are. Chloe's voice is one of those—she doesn't hide her pain; rather, she finds purpose in sharing it. Anyone reading this book will begin to see that personal heartbreak and pain can often lead us toward our greatest strengths and triumphs. Her story is a brave movement of love, one that we can be a part of if we dare to stand beautiful in our own way."

Brooklyn Lindsey, author, speaker,
and founder of the Justice Movement

"This is a must-read book for all victims of abuse/bullying and their abusers/bulliers. It is also a must-read for all individuals with physical differences *and* their health care providers. Chloe's message is pertinent and timely. Her communication style is eloquent, engaging, and endearing. This book has changed me; I believe I will be a better doctor for having read her words and for considering this outcome measure not found in any published clinical research article that I have written or read. We, as health care providers, cannot make everything normal, but we can and should be better attuned to the difference between medical 'success' and patient life experiences."

Vincent S. Mosca, MD; Professor of Orthopedics
at the University of Washington, and Pediatric
Orthopedic Surgeon, Chief of Foot and Ankle Service,
and Director of the Pediatric Orthopedic Fellowship

"Chloe's personal journey inspires us to not give up, to know that we are not disabled but enabled, and that it's not about how we show up but how God shows up in us. Her story emboldens us to embrace God's work within us—that in the midst of pain, isolation, and hurt, we can stand entirely and fully beautiful!"

Mike Romberger, President/CEO, Mount Hermon
Christian Conference Center

STAND
beautiful

A story of brokenness,

beauty and embracing it all

CHLOE HOWARD

WITH MARGOT STARBUCK

ZONDERVAN®

To my parents:
Thank you for standing
beautiful even before I could.

To Tucker:
Thank you for making
every part of my crazy
life full of fun.

Contents

Introduction

"HEY, CAN YOU COME HERE for a minute? I have to ask you something."

I recognized Cece—and her long, dark brown hair—from our sixth-period gym class. Her locker was near mine. She'd paused at my lunch table, where I was eating in the quad with a massive group. I was almost finished with the turkey sandwich my mom had packed in my lunch that morning.

"Sure," I answered. I set my sandwich down on the plastic wrap, stood up, and brushed all the crumbs off my lap. My mom was going through this gluten-free stage, so we only had gluten-free bread for sandwiches. And it crumbled like sand. Not ideal when it came to making good impressions.

I've always been shy, so even though I'd made a couple friends during my first three months of high school, I was having a hard time meeting people. Having someone like Cece reach out to me was a surprise. I, of course, was honored. She was in the achievably-cool group, and I hoped this was the moment they'd invite me into their achievably-cool lives and accept me as one of their own. I so longed to be wanted.

And I got that feeling of being wanted when she beckoned again, nodding her head toward the long, dark blue, rectangular table next to mine. "Come over here."

I began to make my way over to her table, where seven or eight other girls were sitting. I knew some of them from classes we shared, and they were all freshmen, like me. But I was nervous—I hadn't really talked to any of them before. But I pushed that anxiety aside. This was my moment to shine. To prove I was worthy of them.

Then Cece abruptly ordered, "Hey, Chloe, take off your shoe."

Sorry, what? I swear birds froze, midair. Everything stopped.

I felt a chill pass through my body as she looked at me expectantly. My arm hairs rose on end under my sweatshirt. My heart started beating faster and my palms were suddenly way too clammy. Scanning the table, I noticed the other girls glancing, as if barely interested, in my direction. They were all waiting for me to respond.

"What?" I asked meekly, sure I'd misunderstood. This was not what I had expected. Why in the world . . .?

"Yeah, take off your shoe," Cece instructed again. She was starting to get annoyed. What had I done? I was so confused.

My pulse raced and my chest was hot fire. I suddenly wanted only to leave and go back to my own table, with my own friends. I felt so small.

I spoke carefully, hoping to navigate a quick and easy exit. This situation could definitely be avoided. But I had to play it cool. Otherwise, they'd think I was weird and might not want to be friends in the future. If I said the wrong thing, I'd never be in their group.

"Nah, I'm good," I answered, looking at the ground. "My toes are cold." I quickly glanced upward to see if they bought it. My teeth began to chatter. I was so nervous.

"Just take off your shoe," Cece commanded. Then, turning to the group of girls at her table, she proudly announced, "She doesn't have any toenails."

Cece now had the interest of the other girls at the table.

My heart pounded, and my mind started to slow down. This couldn't be happening. People don't just *say* things like that. I felt tears threaten behind my eyes, and my temples seemed to press deep into my head. My hands shook, and my lip quivered in a way I hoped they wouldn't notice. But I had to be strong. I had to brush it off and I had to look poised. Unaffected. Invincible. Untouchable.

"No, I'm okay, I'll leave my shoes on," I wanted to say firmly. But it didn't come out very firm-sounding. I could barely form the words. I couldn't even look Cece in the face. I tried to get my legs to move away, to walk back toward my table and rewind and drive down this hill and not get out of bed this morning.

"Take off your shoe," she repeated.

And for a third time, I said, "No, I'll leave it on." While the words came out clearly, I could barely hear my own commanding voice. I laughed nervously. They didn't think it was funny. It wasn't funny. None of it was.

"Fine," Cece barked, "I'll do it."

She dropped to her knees and began clawing at my shoe, trying to force it off. I pressed my left foot as hard as I could into the ground so she couldn't remove it. My heart was beating dangerously fast, and all I could hear were my loud and rushed inhales. I was so embarrassed. I didn't want to be The Freshman Who Freaked Out in the Middle of the Quad. I had to spend the next four years here. I was so stupid. Why'd I come over here? Why hadn't I just stayed at my table? I stood there and stood there and stood there, my eyes darting around to see if any upperclassmen were looking over. I stood there, trying to look nonchalant. I stood there, biting the inside of my cheek and clenching my teeth and focusing on the ground so I could try and ignore what was happening. I stood there, not able to ignore what was happening.

"No," I said again. But my voice remained so much more powerful in my head than it was out loud. I felt my face burn as I looked at the other girls at the table, who were, again, barely paying attention. Why was Cece *still* trying to get my shoe off? I lost track of how much time I'd been there. As I was becoming tired of it all, almost bored of it, I felt her finger start to slide under the bottom of my shoe, and I stepped down hard. She looked up at me angrily, and then went back to my shoe. She untied it completely. It was going to take so long to rethread the laces.

"No . . . don't . . ." I pleaded. I sounded whiny. Ugh. I was struggling to simultaneously keep Cece from ripping off the shoe that covered what I wanted hidden and still act all cool and composed so the group of girls watching wouldn't think I was weird. It was exhausting. The big feelings of confusion and betrayal and guilt I had earlier had subsided and just left me feeling tired. Heavy. Empty.

As Cece continued to clutch at my shoes, I started to lose my balance and grabbed for the table to steady myself. It was almost funny how terribly awkward this situation was. Almost.

I looked back toward all the girls as they silently watched me. This was getting old. And my foot was starting to hurt from putting so much weight on it. My left thigh was cramping and starting to shake. My brain couldn't formulate words, thoughts. I was watching everything happen to me and consciously knew that what was being done to me wasn't right, but I felt completely removed from the situation.

Allie—a tall, thin girl whose long, bleach-blonde hair was pulled back in a French braid—broke form and walked around from the opposite side of the blue metal lunch table to stand next to me.

"Fine, I'll help," she sighed. This all felt very dramatic to me, but the girls seemed almost annoyed this was still going on.

I didn't even have time to process what she said. Allie grabbed me from behind and wrapped her thin arms around my trunk. She was lean, but strong. Squatting down, and straightening back up, she restrained and lifted me so Cece could take off my shoe and sweaty sock. My arms were stuck to my sides. I was fully and completely frozen. Immobilized. Without saying anything, I watched my little foot be uncovered and held up. My mouth was dry, my eyes weren't blinking, I wasn't really seeing or breathing. I could only stare straight at *it*.

My foot looked so little in Cece's hands.

The other girls leaned in closer to see.

The sounds of the quad and all the people chatting and eating lunch grew quieter until they disappeared. All I could feel was breath on my neck, Cece's hot hands on my foot, and the arms wrapped around me.

"Wow," girls commented in unison. "How'd that happen?"

"Did it hurt?"

"Has it always been like that?"

They pummeled me with questions.

Scars from four surgeries were exposed for inspection. Five toes, four of which are without toenails, became entertainment for others' eyes. Some girls had their mouths open, staring at my foot like it was simultaneously the most interesting and disgusting thing in the world. All I could do was stare. It was like I was looking at my left foot with new eyes. I'd never seen it before in this light. And it was confusing. I looked at the scars from those four surgeries and the tight etchings in the skin they made, curling all over and distorting my previously innocent foot. I saw this foot and I wasn't proud. I was annoyed. Hurt. Betrayed by my own body.

Tipping my gaze away from the girls' faces, hot shame washed over me.

Numb, I quietly, too quickly, answered, "God made me that way. I was born with a clubfoot, and not a typical clubfoot at that. It's just how I've always been." For the first time in my life, I seriously considered how I'd always just been able to accept those words.

When everyone had gotten a good look at my foot, Allie released me. I picked up my sock and shoe off the ground, paused to sit on the emptying lunch table bench and quickly put them on, then returned to my own table. With my own friends. Just six feet away.

Because they kept talking and eating, I didn't know if the people sitting at my table had seen what had just happened. I finished my turkey sandwich. Forced it down. My throat stung. I wondered how red my face was. Conversations continued around me like I hadn't left. I forced myself to laugh along to a joke at our table; I hadn't heard the punch line. When the bell for the end of lunch rang, I carefully packed up, and slowly headed to my sixth-period class: PE with Cece. Great.

I methodically changed into my gym uniform in the locker room, keeping my eyes down. Everyone filtered in, continuing conversations from lunch. I hung around the back corner, pretending to be busy so I didn't need to talk to anyone.

I exhaled for what seemed like the first time in a while when I saw my friend Traci walk in, talking to someone else. I hurried over when she got to her gym locker and waited for my moment. As soon as I could, I carefully and quietly began telling her my story, my eyes darting around to make sure no one else could hear me. "This weird thing happened at lunch . . ."

I told her what I'd experienced, leaving out the names—because that'd be tattling—but she wasn't even looking at me as she quickly changed. Someone yelled across the room, asking her a question, and she answered. Distracted, she said to me only, "Oh, that's weird." Really? That's all?

Our gym teacher announced that we'd be playing dodge-ball in the wrestling room, and that we needed to take off our shoes to protect the massive blue rubber mats.

Nice. Of course this was happening. It was almost ironic.

I dutifully removed my Converse. My little feet were smaller than everyone else's. I fixated on it, studying the normal foot size and wondering how silly my child-sized feet looked on my normal-sized body.

I hated dodgeball.

I moved through the last eighty-three minutes of school in a bit of a haze, unable to shake what I'd experienced. When I filed onto the bus that dropped the high schoolers off at the elementary campus, where my brother was in fifth grade, I felt a wave of dread wash over me as I looked for Cece, who sometimes rode the bus too. I spotted her already seated near the back, talking to some boy I didn't know. I didn't know anyone. I audibly sighed, then slid into a seat a couple of rows behind the driver and leaned my head on the sticky bus window. It always surprised me how the bus windows could be both cold *and* sticky. But all I could really think about was how frozen I had been earlier. The incident at lunch kept replaying in my head, and I felt sick to my stomach. How would I ever live that down? I was so embarrassed. When the bus arrived at Tucker's school, we all piled off and I headed for my mom's silver SUV, where Tucker was already camped in the backseat and talking a mile a minute. Like always, my brother had the unbridled energy and focus of a Ping-Pong ball.

As I climbed in, I answered my mom's daily "How was your day?" with an automatic "Fine." I knew it was the cliché answer for a teenager, which my mom would bug me about later, but I didn't feel like talking. I closed my throbbing eyes. Tucker kept talking and talking and talking, and I relaxed into the sweet familiarity of this daily pattern.

The truth is, I've never really been a typical kid. I usually told my mom everything, from how boring a class was to how my friends were getting along. And she's always known about *all* the boy drama. Not that I had any, of course ("You've got to actually *talk* to boys for one to like you"— Lori Howard, 2013–present day), but she was for sure up to date on everyone else's. Being naturally quiet was good for absorbing gossip.

My mom looked at me expectantly, and I subconsciously adjusted my straight-blonde ponytail, something I do when I'm nervous. Her big blue eyes narrowed as she searched my face, looking for more of an answer, but I didn't know what to say. What do you tell your mom when you feel like a part of you has been exposed without your consent? How do you even begin?

Tucker was talking loudly about some girl in his class, not even caring that we weren't listening, and I was quiet as we drove home. But after about fifteen minutes, I experimentally offered, "Oh, this weird thing did happen today . . ." I was curious as to what Mom would say. Was it really not a big deal, like Traci made it seem?

I proceeded to tell her about the incident at lunch. Emotionless. My mom's pretty aware that I take a lot of time to process my thoughts, but she sometimes gets impatient for more details. And I was sure that would be the case for my current and latest story. But I didn't even try to go into depth, instead simply listed events. I was just so tired.

So Mom's response surprised me.

"What?!" she demanded, her eyes growing wider as her hands gripped the steering wheel.

In that single syllable, I recognized the angry and shocked tone she uses when she comes into my room and sees me on Buzzfeed when I should be doing my homework.

"Wa-wait. Tell me again," she quickly demanded.

When I'd repeated the story for her, narrating just the facts again, she interrupted, "Why didn't you fight back?"

"Uhh . . ." I stuttered, dumbfounded. "I don't know."

What could I say? I was only three months into high school, still on the cliché journey of finding my way and my people. I didn't want to make a big scene. I didn't want to be that new kid who suddenly had a reputation for freaking out. I was embarrassed. I was humiliated. And I was overwhelmed. After I'd said no to Cece *five times*, it became clear that I had no control whatsoever. I wasn't the one introducing my feet to the world. Cece had taken control and Allie had further taken away what control I had, and that was that. There was no consent; there was only power. And it was all theirs. So I froze. I shut down. Even after Allie released me, I still felt restrained. Used. Manhandled. I was numb. I was in shock. I hadn't realized or even really processed that I could fight back in that situation. I was taken aback by Mom's question. Mainly because I didn't have an answer.

"I don't know," I muttered again.

When we got home, my mom had me write down, word for word, what happened and what everyone said. Later, when my dad got home from work, she had me repeat it to him again. All I really wanted was to check out and watch Netflix. I was exhausted.

I had no idea what any of it meant. I had no idea what it would lead to; that it would come to completely consume me and my family.

I had no idea it would change my life.

Like I assume is true for a lot of high schoolers in the rest of the world, I was on my way to figuring out who I was and what I was worth my freshman year. But that whole transformative, feel-good, cry-worthy, "let's make a million and a half movies about it" moment of realizing who you are was sped way up for me. And it happened sooner than it probably should have. A crisis pushed me to immediately weigh and decide what was most true about me. Was I worthy of love and respect, as my parents had always told me? For the first time in my life, I was faced with the possibility that I was not. Ninety seconds I did not choose and could not change forced me to confront the question that simmers below the surface in practically everyone: whether we're worth knowing and loving.

In the days and months after what happened to me, I wrestled to understand who I was and how I was valued. And in the midst of a crazy journey I never could have imagined, I began the process of learning how to stand beautiful.

CHAPTER 1

Congratulations,

YOU'RE HAVING A GIRL

EVERY YEAR ON APRIL 17, my parents tell me the story of when I was born. It's a good one—a story of hope and despair and the power of prayer. It's a good story because it's about not giving up. It's a good story because it's about miracles. It's a good story because it's centered around an unlikely hero. It's a good story because, halfway through my mom's pregnancy, doctors didn't expect me to be born alive.

Until then, everything about my mom's pregnancy seemed normal. She read *What to Expect When You're Expecting* religiously. She and my dad obsessed over buying the right crib, stroller, pacifier—everything. My mom says she puked a lot—which stinks, but is normal. Sickness aside, she was thrilled to be pregnant, and couldn't wait to be a mom. *My* mom. My dad was the same way; he would often put his face right by her growing belly (which soon began to bulge on her tiny frame) and sing to me. Everything was how it should be. Normal.

Halfway through a woman's pregnancy, a mom normally gets a twenty-week ultrasound. At California Pacific Medical Center, just a block and a half from my parents' apartment in San Francisco, my dad watched as the ultrasound technician rubbed the clear gel on my mom. My dad gently stroked her long, straight red hair, they held hands, giggled with excitement, all the stuff you see on TV. It was going to be one of those picture-perfect "put it in the photo album AND on the fridge" moments—until the technician hesitated. She paused the video on a still image, and clicked on the screen to measure. Then recorded her finding. Measured and recorded again. The technician left the room and came back a few minutes later with a doctor by her side. Not. Normal.

When the doctor picked up the wand to interpret the ultrasound for himself, he asked my parents, "Would you like to know the sex of the fetus?"

Of course they wanted to know the sex. Duh.

(It was a girl. They named her Chloe.)

My mom and dad looked at each other, hearts melting a little bit. When my mom heard that word, *girl*, images of dresses, and bows, and ballet recitals, and running in the backyard, and daddy-daughter dances flooded her mind. She looked at my dad, and her face exploded with joy.

As my mom tells it, fireworks went off, balloons erupted from the ground and rose to the ceiling, birds chirped and angels sang.

Without pausing, though, the doctor professionally informed my parents that he saw what looked like two club-feet and a hole in the baby's heart.

My dad is a visual guy. A picture passed through his mind of a deformed foot, of a child who would never walk. Because he'd been a college athlete, he figured in that moment that his child wouldn't play sports. The picture of his perfect little daughter changed in that moment to a broken, disfigured human. He didn't know what to expect. He didn't know how this could have happened—why *they*, of all soon-to-be parents, were the ones who had to experience this. Awash with a sudden feeling of despair, a single word pulsed in his mind: *why?* This wasn't how it was supposed to happen.

My mom struggled to process the words the doctor had spoken. And like many desperate mothers who discover they're having a child with special needs, her mind quickly raced to imagine what she might have done wrong to cause all those problems. She took prenatal vitamins and got plenty of calcium; she rarely drank anyway, and didn't touch a drop during pregnancy; she didn't smoke or do drugs. She didn't even pump her own gas at the station, fearing the fumes would harm the baby. A little neurotic, but okay. She was doing everything right.

The doctor recommended my parents speak with their

obstetrician before leaving the hospital. Even though the doctor's life-altering announcement would eventually give way to an endless number of conversations between my mom and dad, in those first moments, my parents were simply silent.

The obstetrician only confirmed that Baby Me had serious problems.

"I do see two clubfeet," she confirmed, "and also a hole in the fetus's heart." She continued, "I also suspect we might be looking at trisomy thirteen."

The doctor informed them that trisomy thirteen is a genetic disorder where there's extra genetic material in chromosome thirteen, and that children who have this chromosomal defect are most likely stillborn. Or born with severe birth defects.

My parents were heartbroken.

In the months my mom had been anticipating my arrival, she had begun to imagine who I might become. But like my dad's vision of a daughter who played sports, that image faded quickly after hearing about all the problems I'd have.

My mom loves Jesus. And always has. She's always believed that He is good, and has a plan for her, and that He'll show up. Always. But she had so many questions once she and my dad found out that I wasn't going to be a normal baby. She, for the first time, had doubts.

My parents, in their time of distress and confusion,

were sent to all kinds of specialists, all of which referred to me as "the fetus." But it was when they heard the words, "You could interrupt the pregnancy today and no one would slight you for it," that my parents knew they had to just trust that God would pull them through this.

My parents wrestled with why this was happening to them. They asked all sorts of other people to pray for me too. My mom, especially, prayed without end.

God . . . are you listening? Are you here?

My mom's obstetrician had recommended that she have an amniocentesis to help my parents decide what they wanted to do with "the fetus." They could choose to abort, or they could let "the fetus" die on its own and my mom could deliver a stillborn. The options were, in my biased opinion, both complete trash.

A few days before Christmas, my parents returned to the hospital for the "amnio," a procedure where a long needle was stuck deep into my mom to collect amniotic fluid in her uterus, which would help diagnosis any chromosomal abnormalities I could have.

Onscreen, they saw baby me pull away from the needle every time they moved that massive thing around. And seeing me, "the fetus," hiding in the corner of my mom's uterus, moving away from the needle, *mattered* to my mom and dad. Because of their personal beliefs, my parents hadn't really been considering "interrupting" the pregnancy in the first place, but seeing me wiggle away from that needle confirmed their decision. Watching the monitor, my mom saw a little girl who was a fighter, a girl who was going to defend herself against any threat of harm. And she wanted to know that little girl.

Five days after the amnio, my parents got a call from the obstetrician, who confirmed that I did not, in fact, have trisomy thirteen. She sounded really surprised.

"I thought for sure this was trisomy thirteen," she explained. "But all the chromosomes are normal."

Normal. Hmm.

The doctor laughed nervously, commenting, "I guess you just never really know." But God did; after science experiments and tests and giant needles, He proved He had a plan that didn't involve an abortion.

On April 17, 2000, my mom became a mom and my dad became a dad.

My mom went into labor right after she got home from her final prenatal appointment and an hour after my dad went in to work. The story goes that my mom called him and said to "Get home quick, we're having a baby," and that my dad's famous words were, "Okay. Should I take a cab or the bus?" A cab would have been the speedy but more expensive option.

My mom calmly told him that it was okay, he could take the bus, and she'd be waiting for him. I mean, she was going to give birth, it was okay, everything would work out great.

He should've taken a cab.

When he finally got home, they drove to the hospital,

and all was fine and good until it was almost time for my big entrance and my heart rate dropped. Everyone got super serious, because it meant I needed to be born real fast. They ended up—in a moment my dad refers to as "scarring and traumatic"—pulling me out head-first with forceps. The doctor braced herself with her leg on the table and everything.

Knowing about the complicated pregnancy history, the doctor grabbed the phone by my mom's bed and called the baby SWAT team. My mom didn't even get to see me before they whisked me away. My dad watched as the NICU staff hovered over me while they assessed me under the warming light. He always laughs disapprovingly when he remembers that they all looked disappointed that they'd rushed to get there and nothing was seriously wrong with me. Within twenty minutes, they'd all dispersed. I was a healthy baby—I was shown to not have trisomy thirteen, the hole in my heart had miraculously closed, and I only had one perfect little clubfoot. Go me!

I was wrapped in a little white baby blanket, topped with a little pink hat, and brought to my mom. She immediately fell in love with my wrinkled little hands and delicately formed fingernails. Nanny (my grandma) prides herself on the first to discover my seven little missing toenails. And when my mom finally unwrapped me, she discovered my one little twisted foot. The right was perfectly formed, and the left was wrapped around it like an envelope flap. My parents fell in love with my tiny wrinkled feet immediately.

My mother cried happy tears as she whispered in my ear, "It's going to be okay, Chloe Ruth. We'll get through this together." *That's* the picture that went in the photo album. AND on the fridge.

When I hear this story—*every year*—it always ends the same way. "God made you perfectly, Chloe. And He has great plans for you." It gave me my annual reminder that God was there for me before I even took my first breath. And that's pretty crazy to me. My whole pregnancy/birth story is quite traumatic, and maybe yours is too . . . or maybe giving birth to you was the easiest thing your mom has ever done, but I think there's a bigger point. There's a reason I was born the way I was, with all the trauma, tears, and hope, and I don't fully know what the reason is because I'm not God and I can't know everything even though I'd really like to, but I'm interpreting it as a lesson in trust. My parents didn't give up on "a fetus" and they ended up with *me*, a wacky, weird, shy, courageous, loving, curious, not-always-right blonde girl named Chloe. I think there's a reason God allowed me to be here, and I think there's a reason He allowed you to be here too.

It gives me hope every time I hear my crazy birth story. It gives me hope that God will continue to be with me, throughout anything and everything I'll go through in life. Because if God could protect and save a growing little girl who couldn't even *feel* yet, it meant He would be able to protect and save a big girl whose feelings could get in the way of her living. It gave me hope that if things in my life got crazy and confusing and people stopped showing up as support, God would stay with me. Because He stayed before I could even defend myself. How unstoppable would we be together, me and Him? Pretty dang unstoppable, if you ask me.

CHAPTER 2

A SECRET *Superpower*

THERE'S NO WAY AROUND IT: I was born with a left foot that was upside-down and backward. I have a toenail on my big left toe. And no more on that foot; just that one little toenail. My right foot is pretty normal, except that it only has two toenails—one strange, stubby one on the big toe and one more typical one on the baby toe. No one really knows why I only have three toenails, but I like to think of it as God's way of breaking the ice in that whole stressful birth situation. It's as if He gave me something to be like, "Oh, hey, by the way, surprise! I'm not dead and I only have *one* clubfoot, BUT LOOK AT HOW COOL MY TOES ARE." Not that I'd ever say that to anyone in a million years—it's a bit too flippant for my taste—but I like to think that my toes are there for me to share, if I want to. As I understand it now, missing toenails are not associated with typical clubfoot, and I'm okay with not being typical.

I had my first surgery when I was just six months old.

And unfortunately, it really didn't do much except freeze my foot, so even today I can barely point and flex it. I wasn't even a year old, and my foot's functionality had already been significantly diminished. Not ideal.

When I was one, we moved to Seattle for my dad's job. Seattle Children's Hospital was using the newest method for treating clubfeet, called the Ponseti method, so of course we had to see what that was all about. Because kid's bones are so malleable, the Ponseti method uses casting and braces to re-form the foot as the child grows.

Since we were #teamponseti, each evening at bedtime, for three years, my parents strapped me into my "night-night" shoes, which were little white leather lace-up boots that screwed onto a thick metal bar. The brace was supposed to turn my feet outward to straighten my clubfoot, and the doctors were hopeful that it would work. It didn't.

As a result, I had my second major surgery when I turned three, where those poor doctors tried a tendon transfer to fix what had been done in the first surgery. The procedure was actually on my birthday, so the nurses gave me presents: a Barbie doll, a stuffed lamb, and a doctor's kit. There was a therapy dog, a border collie, who laid on a special table set up next to my hospital bed so I could pet him. While that was *awesome*, I was also in an incredible amount of pain. Because all the nerve endings in the body end in your feet, and because cutting into bone makes for deep, deep pain, foot surgery can be one of the most painful kinds of surgeries to have. Lucky me.

Despite being obviously different, and the pain it some-times caused me, I didn't grow up ashamed of my foot. For as long as I can remember, my parents told me that my foot made me special. And I believed them. Honestly, growing up, I felt like I had a superpower—that there was something secret and unique about me that no one else had, that only *I* had the power to share with others. It was, in so many ways, my superpower. Only mine. I was different— and boy, was I proud.

Growing up, I spent a lot of time doing things *differently.* I had my own way of living, and I loved it. I watched cartoons with the cast technician. I had Daddy-Daughter Dates to go see my surgeon. And I wore *so* many casts: blue ones, purple ones, all sorts of casts. To me, it was great. I did *everything* in those things. I drew chalk on the side-walks, I did art, I had Barbie Princess Pony Teaparties™, and I hunted for Easter eggs. Heck, I dragged that purple cast around to look for eggs like no one's business. I *rocked* the cast life.

In a way, casts even became part of my super-powered armor for a while. When I started kindergarten, my doctor tried another round of casting to see if my foot (which was determined to continue to curve) would flatten out more. It had grown very rigid, and it was getting hard to use as a foot. (I'm sure it would've made for a good golf club or base-ball bat or something else hard and unmoving and very un-footlike.) This meant that a few months after my first day in school, I had to show up with a cast. And I chose pink because I was *deep* into my princess/pony/Barbie phase, and pink was THE magical princess/pony/Barbie color. And, of course, I was an instant celebrity because of my pink cast. My fellow kindergarteners were amazed and jealous, and I loved the attention. Tucker, who was two at the time, thought he would like a cast too, thank you very much, so Mom and Dad wrapped his little leg up with an Ace bandage and told him he had to sit still, because that's part of the job. But after 170 seconds, he didn't like that very much, and decided the cast life was not for him. As I like to say, I did not choose the cast life; the cast life chose me. I decided casts were not for the weak of heart, and therefore my pink cast made me a warrior and a hero.

And because I was used to hospitals, doctors, needles, and pain, I was an *expert* caregiver to baby Tucker. He hated getting shots, and when he fell down he would always need a bandage As Soon As Humanly Possible. I became a little nurse to him when he was ill or sad, and would make sure he had Turtle and Bear (his special stuffed animals with very creative names), his blankie, as well as a sippy cup full of juice and a snack of fishies. I would sit next to him on the floor and watch his favorite movie, *Finding Nemo*, patting his little blond head every now and then. I liked taking care of people, and realized I wanted to be a doctor someday—a pediatric orthopedic surgeon like all the ones that'd helped me. It just *made sense*. When people started asking what

I wanted to be when I grew up, I stopped saying "a Barbie princess pony vet" and started saying "a pediatric orthopedic surgeon." And that was my answer for a very long time.

As I grew older and began to get more and more opportunities to share about my foot, I started to see my superpowers in a new light. I realized the importance of my role as storyteller—as someone who could share my experiences to help other people better understand. There were times—at the right place, with the right people—that I really liked talking about my clubfoot. And it was always awkward and didn't feel right when it wasn't my choice—when I didn't choose the time or the place or the people. Letting me share my story on my terms felt like an act of human decency that didn't need to be ordered.

Except when it did.

My family and I were used to the honest questions. Whenever a kid at the playground would notice, "Hey, you don't have toenails," or an adult would ask, "What happened?", my mom or dad would answer matter-of-factly.

"She was born that way."

"She has a clubfoot."

"She's just our Chloe!"

So when I was asked, "How'd that happen?" or "What's wrong with you?" or "Why don't you have toenails?", I just responded like I'd been taught to. To answer matter-of-factly. To be proud; never ashamed.

"I was born this way."

"There's nothing wrong with me, but I was born with a clubfoot."

"I was born with just three toenails. But it's okay."

In first grade, though, I told one of my friends about my foot, and later that week at recess I discovered that she'd told someone else about it. So when another girl came up and asked me about my foot, with a look on her face that was a cross between disgust and curiosity, it didn't feel right. I was happy sharing about my foot with others; the story was mine to tell. But it wasn't meant for friends to use as ice-breakers or playground gossip or stories for Show and Tell. It didn't feel good to me.

And neither did the assault.

But that comes later.

I often struggled to fit in because I was always the "different" girl; the one that showed up in casts and on crutches and sometimes physically couldn't participate in PE. And as I got older, those casts stopped being my superpowered armor and started setting me apart in a way I saw was bad.

Although I'd stopped playing team sports in fourth grade, when I got to middle school I wanted to try doing something new, so I joined the running club. I hated running (and could barely make my foot work the right way), but I wanted to prove to myself that I could be normal, and so two times a week I met my teammates at seven in the morning before school to run around the neighborhoods and do sprints.

And it was trash. I absolutely hated it. But I did it, twice a week, for a full year. Every Tuesday and Thursday morning at seven.

I complained about it so much that my mom was like, "Chloe. What the heck. Just stop doing it if you hate it so much. It hurts your foot and it's hard for you to wake up so early, so just quit." And yes, Mom, all those things were true. But it was so important to me to be a typical kid that I'd push myself, beyond my limits, to do what everyone else was doing. While any of my doctors would have written a note that would have gotten me out of running, period, I always tried my hardest to do what was expected of my peers. And then some. Hence, morning running club.

Up to this point, my clubfoot was my God-given "out." My escape card, my ticket to "special" things. But it was a card I very rarely used. Instead, I lived with a constant desire to know what it was like to ignore that "out" for a while. To see if I was even capable of doing the normal things like PE and running and jumping and all of that, because I needed to *know*. I at least had to try. To know what I was missing. It's like that infamous kid everyone's heard about but no one knows personally who ate a peanut-butter cookie even though he's deathly allergic to peanuts. Stabbed himself with the EpiPen and everything before taking his big bite. Because he *had* to know. Even though he knew it'd hurt him.

I *had* to know.

People don't always get that I live with daily pain. If I sleep with an extra blanket on my bed, the weight of that blanket will press down all night on the top of my left foot—which doesn't bend—and in the morning, it hurts. Other days I'll wake up pain-free, but walking or running, or even standing for too long is incredibly painful. Most days when I get home, my legs and feet are pretty sore. The days when my foot hurts the most are when we have an activity planned: Disneyland, taking a hike, walking through a museum, or standing at a concert. I have to take Advil before, during, and after things like that, as well as ice afterward.

But I was realizing that, even though I'd seen my foot as this incredibly special superpower while I was growing up, as I got older it became less about merely being different and more about everything else. All the pain. The logistics of surgeries, which I had more of: one when I was nine, one in eighth grade, and one in ninth grade. And it was really hard. There was just *so much* pain. I felt like surgeries, in that period of my life, were always imminent. The flexibility issues with my foot were still an issue, and still gave me pain, so I had this massive osteotomy (repositioning of the bone) and fusion to try and fix it, and it just didn't take the pain away. And then I had two knee surgeries to shorten my right leg because it was longer than my left, like for some reason God thought I'd be able to handle more pain and more hospital time and more wheelchairs. But it was hard. And I didn't feel like I could handle it.

I mean, there were *some* good moments. Some funny memories. The time Tucker and I had a race, him on foot and me in my wheelchair—he remembers it wrong, but I was totally the winner. There was also the time my surgeon asked if I had any last-minute concerns, and all I could focus on was the fact that—by whatever surgical law states it—I couldn't wear any underwear during my surgery. (You would've been concerned too.)

But overall, my foot had become this burden in a way it hadn't been before. Not only did I live in this world of forever pain, my foot hurt me on the inside too. As all the other middle schoolers were searching for themselves and finding their place in the awkwardness that defines middle school, I was searching for acceptance and meaning in my life and foot and situation in general. It wasn't just some *cool* thing anymore, or something I could deal with as long as I worked hard—it was this battle that I fought with my own body, every day.

I eventually got past my frustrations, and am learning to live with the pain because I can't do anything about it. It's my *normal.* And we all have separate realities; a different "normal." Which is perfectly okay. What makes us unique—diverse, special, separate, interesting, beautiful— gives us each a new perspective. A distinct set of skills. An emotional advantage. And we have all these things, I believe, for some greater purpose. Some big great reason

God has waiting for us to find. We're all different—and our differences become our strengths when we allow them to.

I was born with a clubfoot. I've had surgeries. I don't know the full and complete reason why, but, in real time, I feel like I may be figuring it out. I am slowly realizing that the pain I've dealt with is actually what gives me strength. I've learned and grown *so much* because of my clubfoot. Because of the surgeries I've had and the pain I've endured. And I can look back and clearly see that even though the surgeries have been hard, and my life hasn't been the easiest, and I live with the constant pain and a desire to just fit in for once, I'm able to turn the burden of having a clubfoot into a superpower. My *true* superpower. When I recognize that I am not disabled but *enabled,* I say yes to God using the superpower He's given me for good. And I'm able to embrace that superpower like no one's business.

We ALL have some secret special superpower. And part of the responsibility of having a superpower is sharing it with others. Clark Kent became *Superman.* He was given superhuman powers and sent to Earth for whatever reason, but those powers would've been completely wasted if he just ignored them, or tried to hide them or hide *from* them. It would've been a totally missed opportunity. And it's the same type of missed opportunity if you don't do something with your secret power. Whether it's your introversion or your extroversion or your compassionate heart or your incredibly loud voice, God gave *you* that superpower! It's *your* special secret thing. Use it.

But who knows. You might come across people that'll try and abuse your secret, special thing.

And then, if that happens, only you have the power to stop them.

CHAPTER 3

SCHOOL OF MY *Dreams*

LIKE THE REST OF THE entire world as their eighth-grade year is coming to a close, I was pretty excited for high school, not going to lie. But unlike the rest of the world, I'd *loved* middle school, and loved who I was there. Although I was naturally introverted, once I just let myself be my normal self I'd discovered that I was funny, and I'd made friends, and therefore I felt pretty good about myself. I mean, I was awkward like all the other middle schoolers, but I felt safe. And seen. And wanted.

One of the big decisions I'd had to make was what high school I was going to go to that next year. The local high school, Los Gatos High, was only an eight-minute walk from my house. And it had a pretty good reputation. I knew people who were going to go there, and I felt like I'd walk in and instantly have people I connected with, and be accepted. But I'd also applied to Canyon Christian, and had heard really great things about it as well.

Canyon Christian High School was big for a private school. My family and I had taken a tour and everything, and I could totally see myself there, surrounded by people exactly like me: people who loved Jesus and wanted to talk about *real* things, not just surface-level stuff. I knew that many of the kids who went to Canyon High came straight from Canyon Christian Middle School, but I was hoping that they'd welcome me in. God was important to me, and I pictured Canyon as the ideal Christian community.

But when I finally filled out the online Canyon application, and clicked to submit the essay I'd worked on for a *long* time, I still wasn't completely sure I'd made the right decision. I, the queen of doubting everything, of course worried I'd made the wrong choice. But I told myself I just had to sit back and trust that if it was part of God's Big and Fantastic Plan for me to go there and meet the people and take the classes and be in that environment, He'd allow me to get in. And then I'd know for sure. No need to look back.

My choice was confirmed when I got a personal voice mail from the principal of the school. As I pressed the play button on my mom's cell phone to listen to the message, I felt like everything was falling into place. This was how it was supposed to be.

"Hi, Chloe, this is Principal Quaid. I personally read your high school application," he continued, "and I loved it. You are going to make an amazing addition here at Canyon Christian, and I am honored to welcome you to our campus as a Crusader."

Until that moment, I'd felt completely overwhelmed with the pressure of choosing between Los Gatos and Canyon. This voice mail was just what I needed—I felt chosen. Accepted. Wanted. This school was made for me. It was obvious. And it felt as good as middle school.

I woke up for my first day at Canyon at 5:30, feeling nervous and excited. I got dressed (three times—duh. I was a freshman. How do you dress like a high schooler when all your clothes belong to a middle schooler?), washed my face (#teenacne), ate breakfast way too fast, and was in the car by 6 a.m. to catch the 6:25 bus that drove from the elementary school to the high school.

I got this.

Honestly, I was probably the world's most prepared freshman. I studied the movie *High School Musical* like it was the Bible, taking mental notes on cliques and boys and finding your way. I knew how to react in any and every situation, and that breaking into song was a great way to solve conflict. High school was going to be awesome. I could feel it.

Several weeks into school, even though I'd had some awkward moments (like walking into the wrong first period on the very first day of school, or tripping down the stairs, or accidentally going through the day with my fly unzipped, or waving back to some guy who wasn't waving at me to begin with), I still felt like I was in the right place. One of the things I liked most about Canyon was that we had chapel once a week. It was always in the gym, where all 1,400 students took over the bleachers and the floor to listen to guest speakers who'd come and talk about Jesus. We never really knew what we were getting ourselves into—that week it could be a well-known comedian they brought to campus, or it could be some random forty-year-old man trying too hard to relate to us troubled youth. During the first week of school, we heard from Principal Quaid, and during the third week they brought in this guy named Nick Vujicic. Nick, who's originally from Australia (which made him cool from the beginning) is an author and motivational speaker, and has no arms or legs. I liked him immediately. Even though I have all my limbs, I saw myself in him; we were the same. As a slightly normal person with a slightly abnormal body, I felt represented in front of all those students and, hearing him talk, I was proud.

Also, he was *really* funny.

At one point, Nick talked about what it was like for him to be in school. He explained, "The big thing that I had to face was all the taunts, all the name-calling. And people pointing their fingers at me, and not playing with me. They thought it was fun to tease the kid without limbs." I don't get why this is a reoccurring theme in schools. (It's really *not* okay to tease anyone—much less the disabled kids—but more on that later.)

"If I was at this school," he asked, in a more serious tone, "would you tease me?"

It was a rhetorical question, but he answered it himself. "Maybe. Maybe not."

He wanted us to know what he knew: even good, privileged, private-school Christian kids can be mean.

He also destroyed the myth—which some people believe—that says that bullying somehow makes kids "stronger." (Silly, silly people.)

He announced, "Bullying makes you weaker. It makes you think more about the negative lies. 'Well, we're just having fun.' Well, it ain't fun for me, and at my expense, you're having fun."

I couldn't imagine anything like what he'd gone through happening at Canyon. *I* wouldn't have bullied him. And I didn't think it would happen at our school. I didn't think it *could* happen at our school.

But Nick also had compassion for those bullies. He said that you don't know what's going on in the heart and mind of someone else. You don't know what they're facing at home. Which is true, I guess. I didn't know how to feel about that, though. Bullies are always bad. That's what I'd always believed. How could you possibly forgive someone who was so awful to you? *So what* if they're dealing with something at home? They bullied someone else, and there's no excuse for abuse (™ Lori Howard, early 2000s). It didn't make sense to me. I didn't think it ever would.

He started sharing what was in his mind all the times

people teased him; all the lies he started to believe about himself. "Nick, you're not good enough. Nick, just give up. Nick, you'll never get a job. You'll just be a burden to your parents. You won't get married . . ." And I could only think about my own life. I began to hear the lies I always told myself late at night, when I worried. "You'll never have a boyfriend. You'll never get married. No one will ever want you." I mean, I *know* that those things probably aren't true. But sometimes those lies really get to you.

Before the end of his big chapel presentation, Nick asked everyone to close their eyes and put their heads down for a little survey. He asked us four questions:

Have you ever considered suicide?

Have you ever tried suicide?

Have you tried suicide because of abuse at home?

Have you tried suicide because of bullying at this school?

I answered no to all of them.

And I was really surprised by his questions. I know it sounds ignorant, so judge me if you want, but I assumed that all the kids who were abused and bullied and suicidal were somewhere else. No way did they go to a school like Canyon.

After the survey was finished, and he'd asked his seemingly inappropriate questions, he said quietly, "One out of five students in this school have thought of committing suicide." Nick paused. No one breathed. "Is that higher than you expected?"

I didn't get it. I couldn't imagine being so desperate that

I'd want to take my own life. My mom had always told me that suicide wasn't even an option; that there are *always* other choices. And again, let the judgement roll in, but I felt smarter than that one-fifth of the Canyon Christian population—they obviously didn't understand the importance of their own lives.

"In this school, there are about twelve or thirteen people who have actually tried to commit suicide."

I shook my head in disapproval, not believing that there were people in this room who would choose to play with their own lives. It just didn't make sense.

He kept going.

"I think there are about three or four out of that twelve who have tried to commit suicide because of abuse at home."

What? The families who sent their kids to Canyon were perfect Christian families. It never occurred to me that maybe they weren't so perfect.

"And," he finished, "about nine, at this school, have tried to commit suicide because of bullying at Canyon Christian."

Sorry. What?

He obviously sucks at counting. Bullying at Canyon?

Impossible.

But if Nick had spoken at my school just a few months later, my reaction to his questions could have been very different. I wouldn't have been so shocked. And I wouldn't have seen myself as smarter than one-fifth of my classmates. I would have gotten it. Understood. Because I would've needed to say yes to Nick's first question.

You know, I feel like sometimes we get lost thinking that everyone's lives are just like ours. Like, everyone has a mom who does their laundry (like mine), or everyone's dad gets up in the morning and goes to work (like mine), or everyone has a little brother who can sometimes be awesome and fun, and sometimes The Most Annoying Person Who Walks the Planet (like mine, #ilovemybrother). I still very much believed that everyone had a life like mine as a fourteen-year-old freshman. I thought everyone was *just* like me. That there would be no reason on earth for anyone to ever want to hurt themselves because they felt too lonely and sad. I had never felt that way and, therefore, it was almost unthinkable that anyone else could ever feel that way. But when I began my journey of suffering in silence, I realized how pain can burrow its way into your heart and make everything that once seemed good and happy and light suddenly an exhausting, bleak reality. And this new knowledge opened me up to the fact that so many people are hurting. And they could be suffering in silence like I did.

CHAPTER 4

"Victim"

I WAS ASSAULTED SEVEN WEEKS AFTER Nick Vujicic visited Canyon Christian.

The evening of the incident, after I'd written everything out in detail for my mom, I wrote an email to the school guidance counselor. I knew her, liked her, and wanted her on my team. After I wrote that email, every part of me was done. Finished. I was exhausted beyond belief and, in that moment, I didn't have enough energy to *feel*.

That night, after dinner, I cried myself to sleep.

When I got off the bus on Monday morning, feeling like I hadn't slept all weekend, I went to speak to my guidance counselor, who'd read my email and wanted to hear exactly what had happened. And after speaking with her, I felt like I was being taken care of. That I'd been seen and heard.

But then later, she popped her head into my math class and interrupted my teacher from the doorway. "We need to see Chloe for a little bit." I was mortified; I hated being called out in class. I slowly got up and, head down, face red, followed her out of the classroom.

She led me to the school security office, which was lined with monitors from the school's camera system. Two uniformed police officers were waiting to speak to me, and even though I knew I hadn't done anything wrong, I was suddenly incredibly nervous. And, strangely, felt guilty.

That was the first time of many that I felt guilty. When I wasn't to blame.

When the officer finished taking notes on my description of what happened, he paused to speak to me directly.

Looking right in my eyes, he said, "You have been the victim of a crime, Chloe, and that crime is called assault."

His words felt heavy. I looked down at my lap, processing. I suddenly felt naked—too vulnerable.

"If this had happened to my daughter, I'd be really, really angry."

I didn't know how to respond.

"Oh, okay," I stammered, then quietly added, "Thank you."

After I spoke to the police officers, I was taken to see Principal Quaid, and I could tell he was angry. He apologized for the fact that this had happened to me, and let me know that the girls had already been sent home.

"We don't know if they'll ever come back," he offered.

Then he added with his too-white smile, "We just want you to heal and have a great Thanksgiving."

"Thanks," I said, genuinely grateful.

I texted my mom as I walked down the hall back to math: "The police just asked me questions."

Send.

My parents were shocked that I'd been interviewed by the police without them present. I'm a minor. I had no idea what I'd walked into.

By the time my parents arrived on campus, frantic and fired up to go to battle for me and my rights as a human, I was already in my next class. So they went right on ahead and had this big meeting with Principal Quaid that they told me about afterward.

"I can't believe anyone on my campus would do this," the principal had begun. "There's no place for this."

An edge of righteous anger rang in his voice, and it was clear he took the matter very seriously. He explained that the girls had been read their rights and interrogated by the police. He said that when the girls' parents had come to take them home, they were really angry.

And that made me feel bad. I didn't want the girls' parents to be mad at them. I didn't want to cause family drama, and I didn't want what had happened to be hard on the girls. Although I'd been the victim, I still felt remorseful for making it such a big deal. I didn't want to be the tattletale that got them in trouble. It was *my* fault that their parents were most likely mad at them. I was responsible.

Principal Quaid nonchalantly mentioned that the whole incident had been caught on security camera, and asked my parents if they wanted to see it. They did. He opened it and clicked play, and my dad squeezed my mom's hand as they braced themselves to watch what no parent would ever want to see.

Though the film was a little grainy, and slightly far away, they could see when Cece came to my table to call me back to hers. They could see me following her. Though they couldn't hear it, they could watch our conversation play out. They could see Allie physically restraining me. They could witness Cece removing my shoe and my sock. They could see her holding up my foot for inspection. They could view the other girls leaning in for a better look. They could see Allie releasing me. They watched me silently put my sock and shoe back on. They could observe that everything I had told them was true. And it broke their hearts.

What they also noticed, though, was that after protesting and being ignored, my body went completely limp. I froze. I shut down. It was the dissociation my mom had heard in my voice when I first told her about the incident in the car, and it was a "shut down" that they'd witness in me for months afterward.

Unauthorized tears streamed down my parents' cheeks as they watched it all happen on Principal Quaid's computer screen. Seeing my assault in that security footage made it real for my parents in a way it hadn't been before.

Principal Quaid shared with my parents that the girls might be expelled, and he assured them that they could rest and let him take care of it. At the end of their meeting, he handed them a small slip of paper with a citation number on it, as some form of proof that the police had come to the building. And so my parents left, feeling confident that the school was taking the matter seriously.

Monday, after school, I rode the bus to Canyon Elementary like I always did. My mom picked Tucker and me up like she always did. Everything, to those looking in, likely felt like it always did. But *I* didn't feel like I always did. As we drove home that afternoon, I felt *different* than I had on the drive to school. The words of the police officer kept spinning in my head:

You have been the victim of a crime.

That crime is called assault.

If this had happened to my daughter, I'd be really, really angry.

I was terrified. What did this mean? How would it change me? I felt like I was suddenly thrust into something big. Too big. Something overwhelming and dark and . . . *big.* Something I didn't want to be a part of.

Victim. Crime. Assault.

As they nestled into my heart and mind, those words felt wrong to me. Dirty.

The one word the officer had used that I didn't yet understand was *angry*. I'd seen anger in my parents' eyes. And on the face of the policeman. And even in Principal Quaid. But I wasn't there yet. For the moment, I was stuck in this world of confusion. Deep sadness. Shame. And guilt.

These feelings signaled my initiation: I was a victim.

The only memories I have from Thanksgiving that year are full of tears, sleep, and endless movie watching. We ended up skipping the big Thanksgiving Day festivities and everything and instead watched *Gone with the Wind* and some Pixar movies. Mom didn't cook. Dad didn't barbecue. And Tucker didn't even play video games. We all simply camped on the couch and didn't take off our pajamas and went into crisis mode. Mom hugged me even more. Dad snuggled me on the couch. And Tucker tried even harder to make me laugh. We all knew that I was *different*. That our family had been changed forever in that one moment. We just didn't know how yet.

Going back to school the following Monday, I just felt heavy. All the time. And though I was quiet before—#introvertsletsgo—I was even more so now. I didn't talk to anyone. As I watched the sea of people moving past me, talking and laughing and texting and flirting, it was like watching a movie featuring people in a place where I didn't belong. Where I wasn't wanted or needed or seen or listened to. It was clear their lives went on, uninterrupted, untouched, while mine felt marked with this "before" and "after." I was changed. Affected. Stripped. New. Different. And no one else was. And no one else knew what had happened to me. No one else knew what I was going through.

I welcomed the end of each school day. The final bell meant I could leave campus on the bus to Canyon Elementary. The elementary school meant I could fall into the safety of my mom's car and finally have someone to talk to. And home meant I could disappear upstairs. My bedroom was and still is my safe space. I feel protected there. And most of all, I feel like me. Like, after a day of pretending, I can exhale. Take off the mask. Let it all go.

I did a lot of staring out the window. Thinking with the door closed. Laying curled in my bed, burrowed in the blankets. Closing my eyes to just listen. I did a lot of my healing in my room, because I could process in that space. And be quiet. I could be me. In a world where I felt I couldn't.

Principal Quaid emailed my dad a couple days after their big meeting, saying that he thought it'd be a good idea for me, Allie, and Cece to all get together for a meeting in his office. He thought it'd be beneficial for me to hear in person how sorry the girls were, and to possibly start moving forward and look toward the start of a friendship.

LOL. Sorry, sir, but what? Friendship? You're out of your mind.

My dad freaked out. He completely lost it even the

thought of me being in the same room as those girls practically gave him an aneurysm. He asked for time and distance for me to process and heal, and told Principal Quaid that it was incredibly insulting to me and to our family that he would even mention the start of a friendship.

My dad later got a call from the principal to let him know the school had reached a decision: the perpetrators, who'd been suspended for just five days, were going to return to campus. Principal Quaid was concerned that the girls' grades might be affected, due to the upcoming final exams, and didn't want them to suffer unnecessarily.

Sorry, they *were suffering? Are you kidding me?*

My dad struggled to understand what he was hearing.

My parents, who really wanted to believe that the school had taken the matter seriously, felt insulted and betrayed. What on earth had happened in the eight days since Principal Quaid assured us all that he would handle the situation, that the girls would most likely not return to campus, and that he would fight for me?

"At our school," Principal Quaid announced firmly, "we believe in grace and forgiveness."

"We believe in grace and forgiveness too," my dad countered, "but we also believe in truth and justice."

And there it was. The great separation between us and Canyon Christian.

I was going to forgive, no doubt about it. I knew from the beginning, from the very moment those girls ripped off my shoe, that I didn't want to carry the weight of those ninety seconds around with me forever. I wanted to be able to, one day when I was ready—let it go. *When I was ready.* I needed my time. I needed time and time and time and then some. I needed time as much as I needed hugs and reaffirming words and feel-good notes in the bottom of my backpack and the reminder that people actually cared about me. And I needed time as much as I needed to not be rushed into forgiveness. I'd been thrust into this deep, dark world where words like *victim* and *crime* and *assault* embodied me before I was ready. So there was no way I was going to be pushed into something without being ready, without preparing for it, without taking a long and thoughtful time to process, and not without *my consent* ever again.

But I needed help. I needed God's grace.

And it got me thinking a lot about who God was in that moment. Would He be willing to let me take the time I needed to heal? Was there some unwritten code that said you always had to forgive someone at circle time on the purple carpet, like in preschool? Was I somehow less of a Christian if I didn't do what Mr. Principal of the Christian School wanted me to do? Would I be able to continue to have faith in a God that allowed horrible things to happen?

CHAPTER 5

Invisible

I'M NOT GOING TO LIE; it's a bit hard to feel confident wearing a knit sweater with big red bows taped to it. But then add the whole "I'm a freshman" inferiority complex to the whole "I was assaulted and don't feel safe at school" thing, and you just have a messy, insecure person. Which was kind of where I was at the week after Thanksgiving, when Canyon celebrated Ugly Christmas Sweater Day. And I didn't own any ugly Christmas sweaters, so I had to make my own. And to make matters worse, if that's possible, I was wearing a bright green rain jacket over it.

I was basically *glowing* with my neon jacket and my metallic bows and my super light blonde hair and my bright red face. I felt like I was on fire.

And still, nobody saw me. I was a walking highlighter, and I didn't feel noticed by a single person.

Because it was raining on that infamous day (poor

freshman neon Chloe and her awkward clothing choices), we all ate lunch in the gym. Which, at least in my experience, was always kind of exciting because it was the *gym* and not the usual lunch spot, and for whatever reason sitting on the gross gym floor or the dirty bleachers was new and fun and not just a gross, dirty high school gym. Maybe you can relate, maybe not. I was sitting at the top of the bleachers with this other girl when I saw Cece for the first time since the assault. If she'd been on the bus that morning, I hadn't noticed her. As the girl and I continued to eat our lunches, Cece began walking up the bleacher steps. And I suddenly *wanted* to be invisible. But instead I looked like the brightest possible version of myself. All I could do was tip my eyes down and will myself to disappear. I didn't want to see her or sense her or think about her, or even know she was there. And I didn't want her to see me. But I couldn't do anything about it. I still had to Keep Calm At All Times because I was a freshman who didn't want some weird reputation for freaking out, and because nobody else at school knew what'd happened to me, and I wanted to keep it that way.

With my eyes at my lap, I heard Cece excitedly greeted by all her friends.

I couldn't finish my lunch.

I've heard that being a teenager is hard enough, but what I was going through, in comparison, felt like utter and complete garbage. It was really hard for me to see Allie and Cece laughing with their friends in the hall, texting all the friends I didn't have, and enjoying themselves like nothing had happened. Allie led the cheerleaders during the school pep rallies. Cece represented the school in Biblical Leadership. They seemed to soar higher in the wake of the assault, while I sunk even lower.

I began to realize that nothing had changed for Cece and Allie.

But everything had changed for me.

I later learned that I was beginning to show signs of PTSD (post-traumatic stress disorder)—which is a big deal—but I didn't know it at the time. Any time I saw Allie or Cece or even one of the girls who'd been at the table, I'd suddenly get really nauseous. Or my heart would start pounding, or I'd get sweaty in weird places or get a bad headache. I'd always turn around and find another route to my next class, even if it was incredibly inconvenient or meant that I might be a minute late to class. I felt uncomfortable and jumpy every day at school, believing one of them could show up at any moment, anywhere, and I would not be safe.

I was guilty because I told, and they got in trouble.

I was guilty because I didn't leave the situation. I didn't fight back.

I was guilty because I didn't forgive them right away—the way that Mr. Principal said I should.

I was scared because nothing was stopping Allie and Cece from retaliating.

I was ashamed because my ugly and abnormal body had been *seen*. Exposed.

I was cautious because I was vulnerable whenever I had to change for PE with Cece.

I was overwhelmed because I was stuck living with this deformity and couldn't do anything about it.

And I was subconsciously isolating myself. Telling myself that I had no one. Believing that I had no one. Ultimately having no one.

There were just three weeks of school left until the end of the semester. Making it through those three weeks of school—riding the bus with Cece every morning, hearing both girls laugh at lunch just six feet away, attending PE with Cece—meant that I always felt on edge. I'd become more cautious than I already was. More guarded. I sat with a group at lunch, but didn't say much. I didn't spend time with anyone outside of school. I just did what I had to. Met the requirements. Lived to the bare minimum.

I began my "sweatshirt phase," where I wore massive sweatshirts to school every day in hopes of hiding myself from the world. I thought if I wore more, I was covered. Protected. Hidden. Safe from being noticed. From being singled out. From being hurt again.

I didn't feel like I could trust people anymore. So, I stopped hanging out with everyone. Some friends knew what had happened to me—that I let people use me and my body, and that I didn't fight back—and I worried that their views of me had changed. That they now saw me as a victim. As voiceless. As unable to stand up for myself. That maybe That Thing That Happened to Me was all they saw. And I didn't want to be Chloe the Victim.

But that's what I was: Chloe the Victim. Because I allowed myself to be.

I grew up pretty sheltered. And by pretty sheltered, I mean the scariest thing I ever saw and have ever seen was the fourth Harry Potter movie. I didn't ever want to swear, and never felt the need to. I switched the radio station if an explicit song came on. I was *that kid.* The kid who, at four years old, ran to each of my neighbors' houses and knocked on their doors and told them that Jesus loved them. The kid who watched VeggieTales when all the other kids were watching Hunger Games (I know, I *know*; I watched VeggieTales with my younger brother until I was in, like, ninth grade. #NBD). The kid who always, always, *always* chose to stay home and have Family Movie Night™ instead of spend time with friends. The kid who criticized the choices my friends made involving dating and clothes and treating their parents poorly because I was *Chloe,* who Knew Everything and Had the Strongest Moral Compass.

But in those ninety seconds of my assault, my experience of reality changed. I had always believed, for the most part, that people are inherently good. But this new reality meant that bad things could happen. And that maybe people aren't good. And, without ever choosing to, I was constantly waiting for the next bad thing to happen.

In those ninety seconds, it was like the giant bandage that had protected my family from what's ugly and painfully real was torn off without our permission, exposing us all to the hard reality we never would have chosen and never would have wanted. One that was completely new to us, and one we didn't always know how to handle.

My dad was mad.

My mom was always crying.

My brother was pretty clueless (like all the other eleven-year-old boys), but did what he could to care for me.

I was quickly rushed into therapy, where I told this perfect-looking lady about all my problems, and she used her careful, quiet, I'm-walking-on-ice voice to console me before she passed the box of tissues my way. Therapy was meant to help me process the trauma and get my life back, and while I didn't like it then, looking back, it did exactly that. The Perfect Lady used words like *PTSD* and *depression* to describe my situation and how I was feeling, and she helped me feel a bit more comfortable sharing my story. Having her as a guide—someone who was not my mom or dad or even someone who knew me personally—allowed me to talk openly and share things I felt I could never share with anyone else. And while the whole confidentiality rule gave me some peace of mind, there was also something about her that made it easier. She helped me see and understand the new me—the me who now had to live in the new reality. And the truth was hard to accept at first; that I was different. That my life was different.

I've never been the person who openly cries when they're sad and yells when they're mad and jumps when they're excited. My dad says I "hold my cards close," which I'm assuming means I keep my bigger feelings—like sadness and anger and excitement—buried deep, deep down. I've gotten better at letting those feelings out with time, but in the months following my assault, it was hard for people to know how I was doing or feeling because, a lot of the time, *I* didn't even know how I felt.

One day I came home after school and, like most days, fell into my bed. My mom sensed it had been a hard day, and followed me upstairs.

"Hey, Cokes?" she asked gently. "Can I join you?"

"Sure," I said, scooching over a few inches. I was sprawled out on my back, and she lay down next to me.

"How are you doing?" she asked.

I forced myself to say a single word: "Okay."

"No, Chloe, how are you *really* feeling?" my mom said with a little laugh as she poked me in the stomach. I let out a little laugh too. Then she got a little more serious and sat up to look me in the eyes. "I know you're having a hard time. I can tell. Dad can too."

"Yeah," I replied, my voice suddenly shaking. Tired. "It's just so hard. Why am I still like this?"

My mom squeezed my hand. "It's fine for you to be where you are right now. I get it. But I also want you to know that you won't be here forever."

"It feels like forever." My voice had gradually gotten quieter and quieter. I sniffled.

"I know. I know it does."

And then she held me as I started to cry.

I didn't understand why God had allowed this to happen to me. I felt like I'd gone through enough already, being born with a deformity and having to go through surgeries and everything. Wasn't that enough? I'd trusted God with my decision to attend Canyon, and my hopes for a place where I could belong had been completely crushed. In fact, the decision I thought had been the best one I'd ever made turned out to be the worst one. I'd trusted God, and now I was left feeling alone. Useless. Trapped.

I didn't know if I'd be able to trust Him again.

Most days, after my dad dropped me off at Canyon Elementary to catch the bus, I'd put in my earbuds and turn on my iPod as we drove up the hill toward the high school. And I listened to the same song every morning on repeat—U2's (RED) single, "Invisible." The lyrics are about not being recognized for who we really are and yet choosing to *claim* who we are and be *seen*, no matter what other people think. Soon, the lyrics became my personal anthem. The words reminded me that, even if people wanted to push what happened to me aside, I was not invisible. I mattered. And I deserved to be seen and known and heard.

Partway through the bus ride to school, the sun would

start coming up. And I was always amazed that there could be so much beauty in a world that had so much broken-ness. And that became my thing: listening to the song that affirmed me most while seeing the beautiful start of a new day. And it made the daily bus rides not as bad.

But as powerful as I felt on those bus rides sometimes, it never lasted. It ended as soon as we drove up that hill and got to campus. As much as I wanted to, I couldn't ignore the guilt and pain; it just wouldn't go away. The school adminis-tration didn't want to deal with me—instead, they acted like they didn't remember any of what had happened, including what they'd promised earlier they would do to help—and the perpetrators' parents seemed to refuse to believe that their children were capable of assaulting me, leaving me to believe what I was experiencing meant nothing. That *I* was nothing.

But my mom would have *none* of that. It was really hard for her to watch me sink into this dark place of pain and depression, and even though I wasn't at the level of anger she was at yet, my mom encouraged me to let out my feel-ings. To not bottle them up so fast and so deep.

One afternoon while I was doing my homework at the desk in my room, I noticed my mom in my doorway.

"Hey," I said, with a flat affect.

"Hey," she began. "How're you doing?"

"I'm okay," I said—my automatic answer.

The expression on my mom's face told me she was unconvinced.

"Chloe, you know it's okay to get mad, right?" She sat down behind me on my bed.

"I know," I said, halfheartedly, turning toward her. I knew I was allowed to be mad, but I didn't really think I was capable of being *anything* but sad.

"Dude," my mom ordered, pointing at my iPod dock, "turn on 'Invisible.'"

All of a sudden, there was this whole new side of her. My mom's the type of person that shows every emotion. *Every* emotion. And at that moment, she was pretty fired up. She stood and was kind of bouncing on her toes as I scrolled through my playlist until I found the song, and as the thumping beat began, she reached over and cranked the volume up all the way.

And then she pulled me up out of my chair. And we started dancing. Jumping, waving our arms every which way, banging our heads along to the drums.

And when Bono began singing that explosion of reaffirming worth and value, we joined him. By the time he'd hit the first chorus, we were screaming our lungs out.

I am not invisible.

I'm not going to say I wasn't a *little* frightened. I wasn't used to seeing my gentle mom having that much anger, excitement, and raw energy all at once. And when I heard her throw in some colorful language that wasn't part of Bono's song, I threw in some too. A lot, actually. And as we were jumping and waving our arms and screaming with that midafternoon sun coming through the dusty blinds, with the door closed and my brother downstairs, it wasn't Bono's song anymore. It was mine.

And those feelings of anger and injustice and sadness that I'd hidden from for so long erupted from deep down in me, and suddenly all those emotions were mine too.

I realized that this world was *mine. My* world was mine. No one else had the power to change my world but *me.*

And it felt good.

I was in for another feel-good moment not long after.

A week and a half before I'd been assaulted, my dad had been scrolling through his Facebook feed when he noticed a contest being promoted by a company called Omaze, which raises funds for nonprofits through online auctions centered on once-in-a-lifetime experiences with celebrities. Someone who donated to a cause and won the contest got to hang out with Robert Downey Jr. on the set of *The Avengers.* One winner attended Ringo Starr's birthday brunch. Another dude hung out with Snoop Dogg in Colorado. And someone else mastered his spiral with Tom Brady. You get it.

When my dad paused to read the promotion, he learned that there was a contest to help (RED), an organization started by Bono that combats HIV in hopes of creating an AIDS-free generation. And the prize was a chance to meet Bono backstage. So he donated and entered the contest.

Because Bono. Duh. But he figured he wouldn't win. (We're the family that never wins anything, ever.) So after he clicked the link and closed the tab, he didn't mention it to me or my mom. End of story. Or so he thought.

Over Christmas break, he received an email saying that he'd been chosen as one of ten finalists for the backstage experience with Bono. Some lady asked him to do a Skype call the next day for background info they could share with (RED), and so he did.

Then while we were on vacation, my dad got a Facetime call. And it was a woman from Omaze. The company's team talked with my dad, and then he had me come in from the pool.

Dripping wet, with a green-and-white-striped towel around my shoulders, I listened to the lady explain onscreen, "So, your dad entered for a chance to meet Bono, and we randomly chose a winner . . ."

My dad looked up at me. He was already grinning.

"And," she continued, "it's him."

My eyes got so wide, I probably looked like a cartoon character.

My dad laughed, "Can you believe it?!?"

No, actually, I couldn't. Like I said, we never win anything. But I couldn't stop smiling. We'd won the thing that mattered.

My dad said, looking up at me, "Now, Chloe, I get to take a guest, backstage, to meet Bono . . ." Biggest smile I've ever seen him have, to this day.

I was stunned. Couldn't speak. My eyebrows raised up so high, I'm surprised I didn't give myself instant wrinkles. I smiled with all of my face.

When we hung up, my dad screamed, "We're gonna meet U2!!!!"

Finally, something was going right.

A week before school started back again for the second semester, Dad grilled some steaks for dinner and we all bundled up so we could sit outside to eat in the January sun. We all ate together and, for a moment, I felt safe—normal.

"Hey, Chloe?" my mom began, as if asking my permission to speak.

"Yeah," I replied.

Sheepishly, she offered, "I want to apologize to you."

I laughed. Then stopped, confused. "Wait, why?" What could she possibly have to apologize for?

"Chloe," she continued, "I'm really sorry for how I responded when you first told me about your assault."

There had been a lot of reactions from people I hadn't appreciated, but my mom's had not been anywhere near the top of that list. At that point, she was in grad school learning how to be a therapist, but she had always been super sensitive and supportive.

I asked, "I don't get it. You've been good."

"No," she corrected me. "I said something in the car that day that I really regret."

I had no idea what she could be talking about.

"The first time you told me about your assault, I asked, 'Why didn't you fight back?'"

She met my eyes and then looked down. She was embarrassed, I could tell. This had really been bothering her.

"Well," I answered, "I mean, it's a good question. It makes sense. I don't think I really could've fought back in that moment, because I was so *frozen*, so in shock, but I didn't think that you asking it was bad. I ask myself the same question. Get mad at myself because I didn't fight back."

"No," she pressed, "it wasn't right for me to say that."

I still wasn't following.

Curious, I asked, "Why not?"

"I mean," she explained, meeting my eyes, "it suggests that you did something wrong. Which you really didn't." Her eyes got real big, the way they do when she's serious. "It's like when a girl gets sexually assaulted by a stranger and then blames herself for wearing the wrong clothes, or sending the wrong signals, or screaming, or not screaming. And I *never* want you to think that you did something wrong. You didn't, Chloe. You *didn't*. And I'm sorry if it sounded like I thought you did when I asked that stupid question."

In that moment, I got it.

"Thanks, Mom. I knew that you were only trying to figure out exactly what had happened. But thanks."

"Chloe," she answered. "You're a pretty special girl."

Jokingly, I agreed, "What can I say? I *am* pretty awesome."

She stood up and gave me a hug, then grabbed a few plates and took them to the sink.

"Who wants dessert?" she asked. We all wanted dessert. She'd bought strawberries, and there was promise of strawberry shortcake. Nobody in their right mind passes that up.

But our good evening took a turn when she reminded me that I had to decide whether I'd return to Canyon at the start of the next semester. I'm someone who's very thoughtful about the decisions I make, and I take a long time to process things. But at that point, I could have made an argument either way. And I knew that this was up to only me to decide, which scared me. The last big decision I'd made had been to go to Canyon, and that didn't turn out too great.

On one hand, there were good parts about Canyon. For starters, I really liked my teachers. I felt that, for the most part, they really cared about me. But I usually felt pretty lonely at school (as we all do sometimes, I'm sure). When I sat with the group at lunch, I always ended up just watching them interact with each other without actually participating myself. And after school, I'd avoid people altogether by going to the library to wait for the bus so I could just sit in the quiet. My mom reminded me that I hated waking up at five thirty. Which was true. Each weekend, I dreaded returning to school on Mondays. And, of course, there was also the assault, which cast a pretty massive shadow over the Canyon campus for me.

After I chewed my bite of shortcake (so good), I finally answered, a little irritated, "Okay, okay. I'll think about it."

I wasn't looking forward to making this decision. It was going to be a hard one. The familiar (but sucky) Canyon, or the new (and slightly intimidating) Los Gatos High.

But then I remembered what had happened a week before the first semester ended.

I was about to enter the gym bathroom when I unexpectedly saw Allie. She was standing by the sinks with one of her friends. It was the first time we'd been in close proximity since the assault, and I was not only alone, I was outnumbered. I was so startled, I think I actually jumped before stopping dead in my tracks right in the doorway. I wasn't ready for this. We looked at each other, and then I dropped my head down really fast and looked at the grimy blue-and-white-tiled bathroom floor. I felt my heart racing, the same way it had felt when I'd seen her in the halls. I quickly walked past her and rushed into a stall and shut the door, sat on the seat, and pulled up my legs. I waited there for more than ten minutes, until I was sure that she'd gone, and I felt tears threatening to sabotage me the whole time. Being so close to Allie made me feel like a victim all over again. Or at least, more so than I usually did. After she left, I washed my hands and peered at myself in the mirror. I looked like a child.

Why was I like this?

After school, when I got on the bus, I chose a seat halfway to the back. I saw Cece get on, and I looked down. And she sat right behind me. *Right* behind me. She had already started sitting closer to me in PE, but doing the same thing on the bus was new. I didn't want to be rude or draw attention to myself by moving, but at the same time I was becoming very nervous. I felt as if I was on fire. My throat was suddenly too dry. My palms were suddenly so sweaty that they were too slippery to hold my phone, so I couldn't pretend to be busy texting. I nervously fidgeted with my ponytail. I felt her eyes all over me. And when the bus driver pulled away from the school, Cece started kicking the back of my seat.

She kicked it the whole twenty-five-minute drive to the elementary school.

I said nothing.

The memory of encountering both girls on the same day made me question whether I could stay at Canyon for three more years. And it made me pay more attention to what was going on in my heart. I wanted to forgive both girls and just forget about the whole thing. Move on. But I refused to pretend as if nothing had happened. That's what the administration was doing, it's what Cece and Allie were doing, and it felt wrong to me. I wanted my forgiveness to be real. And that was it.

I had decided.

I would stay at Canyon for the rest of the year. I *needed* to stay for the second semester. I had to prove that I was stronger than how they made me feel. I was stronger than what had happened to me. So I couldn't escape. Not yet.

I had more to do.

CHAPTER 6

ALL THE BAD *Things*

I KNOW THAT, WHEN I SUNK low emotionally after the assault, my parents felt helpless. They were terrified I'd harm myself in some way, like they'd heard many kids do after going through things similar to what I was dealing with—ways like cutting, drinking, drugs, suicide. There just wasn't that much they could do to help me heal.

One night, my dad walked into my room when I was supposed to be doing homework. I knew he was there, but I didn't turn my head or even really care. I was curled up on my desk chair, writing the word *beautiful* in black Sharpie over the scar that ran along the inside of my left foot.

He watched me for a bit, and then asked, "Is it okay if I take a picture of it?"

"Sure," I agreed, not looking up.

Pausing to look into my eyes, he gently asked, "Why'd you write that, Goose?"

I answered honestly, "I don't really know."

And I didn't know. But I kept writing that word: Beautiful. And each time I wrote those nine letters—four consonants, five vowels—I came to realize I was saying no to the victimization and the stares and everything that didn't make me feel worth it, and saying yes to everything that did. When I wrote that word over my scar, I was calling all my surgeries, all the physical therapy, the insecurities and the ninety seconds of the assault—every single thing—beautiful. And as I spent time with that word, I began to consider what it meant for others. If it was true, if *I* could choose to believe my scarred, twisted little foot was beautiful, then others could too. We could all choose to see ourselves and our society-deemed imperfections as beautiful.

Even though many days it was still difficult to get up and face the day, this little seed was planted in my heart—of finding beauty. Of *choosing* to believe that I was beautiful, foot and all. At first, it was just the one word: *beautiful.* But I wanted *more.* If I was going to invite people to think and live differently, I needed to be able to invite people to action. Eventually, I began to hear two words: *stand beautiful.*

I Stand Beautiful.

I liked it.

My dad knew that I'd been thinking about sharing this message, and the night he took the picture of my foot, he created a prototype website that he showed me a couple days later. He told me that he liked my handwriting, and asked me to create a few versions of the word *beautiful* in my own script. But I didn't know the implications of starting a website, the things that would come from putting my story out to be heard. But in that vulnerable moment of merely opening up to the possibility, a brand was born. A movement was created as that website started to grow. A statement was made and a battle was fought. In that moment, I gave myself the power to change. And that meant everything.

Though I wasn't able to recognize it at the time, creating that website was my first baby step toward healing. It was my first step toward forgiving. My first step toward speaking out. My first step toward saying *yes* to God.

Yes.

I don't know if you've ever experienced this—but maybe you have. The completely empty feeling of knowing that the people who do bad things get away with it. Or seemingly get away with it. There are people who play dirty, ditch friend groups, do anything they can to rise to the top of the high school hierarchy, and *it works* for them. Students cheat on tests, break the law, and somehow never get caught; it *happens.* It all does. And if we're on the other side, we're left feeling empty and alone and worthless. Like we did something wrong, we'll never succeed by following the rules, like no one sees our pain. *We are the unseen.*

But that's just what they try and tell us.

That's not who we really are.

We are seen by the eyes that really matter. God sees us and loves us—and, no, I didn't realize that at the time. Few people do. But I can see now that God is the King of justice. I'm not saying that karma's a thing, because I don't think it is, but I do believe that God doesn't let people get away with their unjust actions. And it might not happen immediately, or within a couple years, or even in a way that we can see, but I truly believe that our God is one who makes things right. And I don't have all the answers. Actually, I have *none* of the answers. I can only tell you what I see and feel and believe in my heart, and I'm trusting that God doesn't want bad things to triumph, so, ultimately, they don't. And sometimes it isn't necessarily about seeing those who wrong you or wrong others get punished—it's about believing and knowing that we are seen and we are worth more. We are greater and stronger than those evil, unjust things that happen to us and around us every day. Because if we follow God's Word, and trust God when He tells us He is our refuge and that He will never forsake us, we can have the assurance the wrongs in this world will be overcome.

While I'd sometimes doubted this promise at times in the aftermath of what happened to me, God sent me a powerful reminder that justice had always been part of His plan—He'd simply been working in the background until I was ready to see what He'd been doing. When the police had come to question me about the assault, a case file had been opened and then left, up for grabs. Nothing happened with it for a long time but, finally, when a California district attorney (DA) got her hands on my case, she was appalled. She'd never seen a case like mine before—one that qualifies for a hate crime without the use of threat of violence or weapons of any kind. Mine was a case of emotional battery, and the DA wanted to fight for me. Once my family and I were connected with the DA, we were notified that both Allie's and Cece's parents hired private attorneys. Preparations began for court, and after a year, we went to trial.

Back in October, I'd been having problems with the metal plate in my knee. Tendons and fluid-filled bursas rubbed against the metal that was separating the growth plates below my knee that had been put in during 8th grade. We had scheduled surgery for April, but because there had been so much going on as we began to prepare for court, I'd forgotten to dread the surgery the way I usually would've. But as March became April, there was no avoiding it. My surgery, the second one I'd had on my knee, was very, very painful.

The surgery came during an odd season. I was healing emotionally from my assault, struggling at school, dealing with the school administration who continued to ignore me, and thinking a lot about God. I was asking hard questions about why God allows bad things to happen to good people. And I became very sensitive to Christian clichés that wouldn't have bothered me before my emotional and physical suffering. Things like *"God has a plan," "You might not see it now, but there's a reason for this,"* and *"Everything works together for good for those who love Jesus"* made me want to punch someone. And cry. And throw up a little.

I hadn't given up my faith in God, but I was becoming tired of the simplistic answers Christians sometimes use to dismiss the suffering of others. And to be fair, I noticed that people who'd actually endured suffering never said these things in the wake of something hard. During my hardest days, the friends and supporters I most needed were those who recognized that I was hurting.

Our DA was fired up from the start. She was incredibly passionate about my case, and even made time to meet with us to help me through the new and confusing process.

Two weeks after school ended (#byecanyon), the DA asked us to meet at her office on a Saturday morning. The Santa Clara County DA's office was housed in a tired, run-down government building, and the DA met us at the entrance, since it was all locked up for the weekend.

She was an African American woman in her mid-fifties, who stood a few inches taller than me. And she wasn't dressed like the typical high-heeled, pencil-skirt attorneys I'd seen on television. At least not that day. She wore a long gray sweatshirt over black yoga pants and, after greeting my parents, she led us up a series of elevators and winding hallways, each one accessed using the ID card hanging from a bedazzled lanyard around her neck.

When we reached her small office, it was littered with

stacks of files on other cases. Rape, murder, sexual assault. As I looked at everything my lawyer had to deal with, she surprised me by saying that when my case finally came to her attention, it had connected with her. It *angered* her. She saw me in a way that other people had a hard time seeing. People asked me, "Why didn't you fight back?", "Why didn't you walk away?", "Why did you just stand there and let it happen?", and even, "They didn't hurt you, though. So, you're okay, right?" But she got it. From the beginning, my DA understood that I couldn't fight back. I couldn't walk away. I was forced to just stand there. And I wasn't okay. She *saw* me. And that support was just what I needed to give me the strength to get through the difficult trial. She was sharp and fierce, and I was convinced that, like my parents, she had my back.

At one of the earliest hearings, a defendant has the opportunity for Deferred Entry Judgment (DEJ), which means that if the accused is a minor and is willing to admit their guilt, they can get about six months of probation. And then it's over, it's done, there's no trial, and it's not a big deal.

But both girls refused to admit their guilt.

Cece's and Allie's families each insisted their daughters were innocent. Their private attorneys approached our DA to make a deal.

"No," she countered, and reminded them of the opportunity to plead guilty and get the DEJ.

They pushed to have the charge lessened to a misdemeanor.

"No," she told them simply, "I'm not doing it."

Because Cece had seen my foot in the locker room two-ish months before the assault, the case had grounds for both prior knowledge and intent to commit a crime. I didn't choose to go to trial. My parents didn't choose to go to trial. But when the girls refused to admit guilt, and the private attorneys refused to comply, the only way forward was a trial.

If Cece and Allie had come forward initially and admitted their guilt, everything would've been better. Easier. But they refused to apologize. Refused to even acknowledge the incident as significant.

Honestly, we never could have imagined that the assault we'd once wanted the school to manage would drag out so long. For months, the case was misfiled in the system, buried so deep that no one knew it existed. Once it was discovered, we spent the summer after my freshman year of high school going to court for pretrial hearings, because the defense attorneys were intent on proving that I didn't have a disability. They thought that if they could somehow prove I wasn't disabled, they could take the hate-crime allegation my DA had pressed for off the table because, if I wasn't disabled, the girls wouldn't have been singling me out for any reason, other than just to be jerks.

But, unfortunately for them, I and the rest of the world know and believe that I have a disability. And I and the rest of the world also know that it's not okay to assault someone because they're disabled.

We had to provide documentation and a testimony from me, from my parents, and from my doctors and surgeons to *prove* I had a disability. I had to write a letter to the court about how "horrible" it is to be me, describing the physical limitations and emotional challenges I've faced because I was born with a clubfoot, and one that isn't typical.

Our DA also requested medical records, interviewed people, did tons of research, and gathered all sorts of documentation to prove I had a disability.

When we asked my surgeon to produce a statement, he laughed and asked, "Is that a real question?"

Right?

During this whole ordeal, I felt 100 percent powerless. Nothing I could say or do would make any of this go away. It felt like we were on a giant merry-go-round—although this ride was no fun. At all. We were just going around and around and around with no change. I began to wonder if this is what the Bible talks about—that life will still be hard even if you follow Jesus. I mean, I'd heard about Jesus and love and all that my whole entire life. But this really sucked. It hurt to be dragged through all of this when all I really wanted to be was a normal teenager.

I wanted my biggest complaints to be about picking out the perfect dress to wear to the dance, or that I didn't have any tan left from summer. I started burying myself in Instagram and Buzzfeed, and tried to numb myself with the amazing lives that other people my age were living. As I continued to immerse myself in that land of make-believe, I felt even more distant from God. Didn't He want good things for me?

CHAPTER 7

VIP TO VIP

THE U2 CONCERT WHERE WE met Bono was in my dad's hometown of Denver.

My dad and I were both, understandably, super nervous. Like, *more* than nervous. I was meeting The Guy Who Wrote and Performed All That Amazing Music I'd Been Listening to for My Whole Life, and my dad was meeting his hero. We really didn't even know how much time we'd have with Bono or whether we'd make a connection. So, yeah, we had so much anxious energy, it was coming out of our ears.

Once there, the evening was a blur of backstage tours and special lounges and VIP parties. But when one of Bono's people came to get us, and asked us if we were ready to meet him, everything slowed down. *Bono.*

Duh. Of course we were ready.

We were led into a smaller room backstage, where we'd

have our little meet and greet. Little; LOL. It felt like the biggest moment of my life. We had to wait there for about twenty more minutes because Bono had such a crazy pre-concert schedule. He's a rock star, so we forgave him.

And then Bono came into our room. He was wearing all leather (even pants, which was beyond cool) and had on gold earrings and pink-tinted glasses (sunglasses? Inside? A whole new *level* of cool). His hair was even bleached a bit on the top.

What a cool guy.

He sauntered over in a way that only Bono can, and shook our hands. From the start, he didn't act like he had someplace better to be—he was super present and seemed to care about us and our interaction. Everything about his posture, his eyes, his smile communicated that we were worthy of his time.

After greeting the other people in the room—including Matt Pohlson (the CEO of Omaze) and a cameraman who was documenting the experience—Bono turned to speak to us, and my dad told him how important U2 has been throughout his journey, remarking, "U2 has really been the soundtrack of my life." My dad told him that the most meaningful moments in his life happened alongside Bono's expanding body of work. He thanked him for being an extraordinary humanitarian, and for using his fame for good. He said he was grateful that Bono was a good role model for the new generation and how happy he was to share this special moment with part of that new generation—me!

"And," he said, still looking at Bono but turning toward me, "This is my daughter, Chloe. She has a story to share with you."

Bono, standing just two feet away, turned and looked right into my eyes. I don't know how to describe it other than to say that he was just so *there*. I expected him to listen and nod, but instead he made me feel like what I was about to say actually mattered to him. Once he locked eyes with me in that moment, he didn't look away.

I began, "I've listened to your music my whole life because my dad has always listened to your music. But this year, your music became very important to me, because I had a really hard year. I was assaulted at my school for a severe foot deformity that I was born with—"

I must have been talking fast—something I do when I'm nervous—because Bono interrupted to ask, "You were *insulted?*"

"No," I clarified, laughing nervously. "I was *assaulted*."

His face flushed with compassion and he said, "Injustice. What happened to you was an injustice."

"Yeah," I confirmed, "It was really hard and really serious. It happened in November, about the time when your new album and (RED) single came out. 'Invisible' really spoke to me. It inspired me to not feel as invisible. And this year it taught me to use my voice and stand up for myself."

And he asked, "Use your voice, like *sing?*"

"No." I laughed again. "Like use my *words* and put power to them. And it changed me a lot this year. So, thank you."

He seemed to mull over what I'd said for a moment, and then offered, "People ask me if I get nervous when I speak to leaders of the world about injustice. No, I don't. Do you know why? Because I am right and justified. And the things I say to them are good and important. They should be nervous to speak to me. It's like a punch. Not a physical punch, but a verbal punch, collected with all the energy of the world. And that makes it powerful."

"I like that." I smiled.

He continued, "The arc of the universe bends toward justice and love."

Whoa.

"When you are right, when you have truth, and tell your story, it can give you that power. You have to use that power to fight injustice."

I was kind of in awe. It was that type of jaw-dropping, Sit and Listen, don't-want-to-leave respect and appreciation and *awe*. Bono was calling me to action. *Me*.

And I wanted to answer that call.

Then he asked me, "Do you have a passion yet?"

"No," I confessed, laughing. Always laughing. I must've looked crazy. But that's okay. "I'm still figuring that out."

Bono nodded, smiling, and confirmed, "That's a good place to be." Then he added, "If you have faith, you can just be open and know that you will find it eventually."

I interrupted, "Well, I love Jesus, and I know you love Him too."

Bono smiled more than he had before, and you could

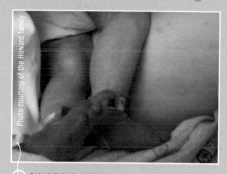

CHLOE'S CLUBFOOT ON THE DAY SHE WAS BORN

CHLOE AT FOUR MONTHS, EXAMINING HER CAST

CHLOE WITH HER MOM AT TWO YEARS OLD, WEARING HER "NIGHT-NIGHT" SHOES

CHLOE ON HER FIFTH BIRTHDAY, DEEP IN HER PRINCESS PONY PHASE

CHLOE AND HER BROTHER, TUCKER, FOLLOWING
CHLOE'S SURGERY AT THE END OF 4TH GRADE

Photo courtesy of the Howard family

HOWARD FAMILY PHOTO, 2015

OUTSIDE THE COURTHOUSE, BEFORE WALKING INTO HER TRIAL TO TESTIFY ON THE STAND

THE FIRST TIME CHLOE WROTE *BEAUTIFUL* ON HER FOOT

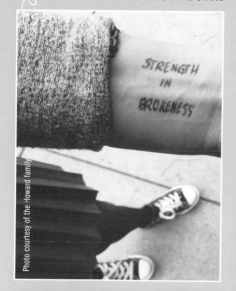

Photo courtesy of the Howard family

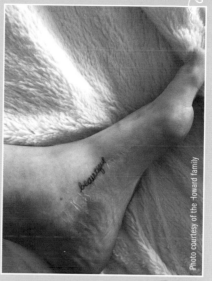

Photo courtesy of the Howard family

Photo by (RED)

CHLOE AND HER DAD BACKSTAGE WITH BONO

fellow comrade
chloe your head
and heart are a
perfect rhyme
your fan
Bono

THE DRAWING BONO SENT CHLOE
ONE WEEK BEFORE HER TEDX TALK

CHLOE ADDRESSES THE CROWD AT TEDX
SANTA BARBARA ON AUGUST 20, 2016

CHLOE MEETING PATIENTS AT A CLUBFOOT CLINIC IN THE DOMINICAN REPUBLIC

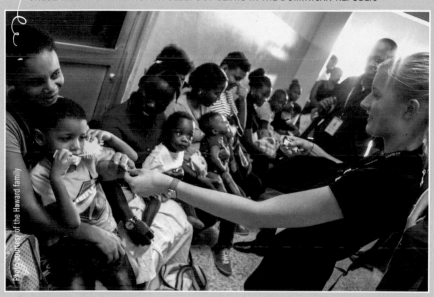

Photo courtesy of the Howard family

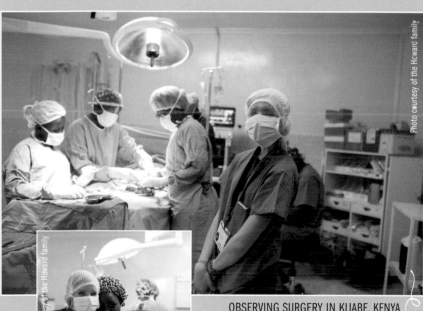

Photo courtesy of the Howard family

OBSERVING SURGERY IN KIJABE, KENYA

Photo courtesy of the Howard family

THE SURGEONS AND STAFF IN KENYA
WERE AMAZING, FRIENDLY, AND JOYFUL.

TALKING WITH JAMES ABOUT
HIS CLUBFOOT EXPERIENCE

REACHING OUT TO A CHILD WAITING
IN THE KIJABI CLINIC

TALKING WITH JAMES ABOUT
HIS CLUBFOOT EXPERIENCE

Photo by CURE International

Photo by CURE International

Photos courtesy of the Howard family

GETTING TO KNOW SOME OF THE FAMILIES
AT THE CURE KIJABI CLINIC, KENYA

Photo courtesy of the Howard family

MARTHA, WHO BRINGS ME JOY.

CHLOE ABOUT TO SPEAK TO A CROWD
AT A FRESNO, CA, CHURCH

CHLOE BESIDE A CHILD WITH SCARS LIKE HERS

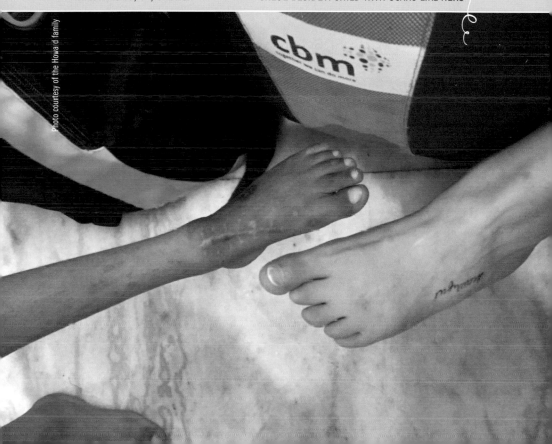

Photo courtesy of the Howard family

CHLOE IN HER CAR, BERTHA, AFTER BERTHA GOT HER FLAMES

Photo by Zondervan

MEETING ONE OF HER HEROES, BETHANY HAMILTON, AT
ANCHORED IN LOVE, GARDENA, CA, 2017

see his eyes turn up under his rose-colored sunglasses as he said, "In my family, we have a prayer. That prayer is, 'Make us available for work.' Now, sometimes we say it among the six of us at home, and sometimes we say it at the pub. But we are always open and available to God, and are always ready to accept whatever He has in store for us."

Then he encouraged me, "You stay available for work, and the work will wash over you."

Dang.

"Wow," I marveled and, remembering what my dad had said, added, "You're such a good role model."

And Bono just chuckled and said, "Oh, if you only knew me!"

I laughed with him (not that I ever really stopped laughing) and said, "Well, it *seems* like you're a good role model, and there aren't a lot of good role models for my generation."

Then his assistant, who'd been glancing at her watch, stepped in to say it was time to take pictures and have him sign the red Gretsch guitar that was part of our prize.

Which was pretty cool, not going to lie.

Bono knelt down by the guitar and signed his name with a Sharpie, and then wrote our names too.

Then he smiled, and added, "I'll make this extra special," and he drew a face on the back. The tour photographer snapped a few pictures of my dad and me with Bono, and we basked in the glory of That Amazing Man in That Amazing Moment before we were escorted out.

It had happened. It was done. It was incredible.

And what Bono had said would forever impact me.

The week after my dad and I got back from Denver, he wrote a note to Bono's people, thanking them for an amazing experience and asking some follow-up questions we'd had since that unforgettable night.

My dad and I had both been curious about when Bono had last played the guitar he'd autographed for me. Was it one he used at home? Had he played it at an earlier concert? Was it from his older albums, or had it been purchased two days prior? Bono's people did some research, and got back to us.

It wasn't a guitar Bono had kept beside his living room piano or in his closet at home. And it wasn't used in the older albums.

It was better.

Bono had last played the guitar that was now standing in my bedroom inside a Dublin recording studio in 2013. He had used it to play the track to a song that would eventually become "Invisible."

My jaw dropped. My dad's eyes got so big, I was surprised they didn't roll right out of the sockets and onto the floor.

If that isn't God, then I don't know what is.

After birthdays and Christmas, my mom usually has to

bug Tucker and me to write our thank-you notes. And it's a process that can take months. If we procrastinate for too long, she'll physically put paper and pens out and sit us down at the kitchen table, then supervise us until we get them all done. But I felt so inspired and challenged after meeting Bono, I really *wanted* to send him a letter to let him know that meeting him had been more than a photo op for me. Something had shifted inside me, and meeting him had *changed* me. Maybe you've had an experience like that too—something that hit you, or moved you, or some conversation with some person that made you feel like maybe you *were* made for something greater. And it's scary. To get that pull to do something or be someone bigger and not know what that means, or how a future living like that would look. But when you start thinking about your life as a series of orchestrated events that have all led you to where you are now, you can see the small ways your life has been impacted by others and by your surroundings. And it's all led you *here*. Right where you are, right now. And I was thinking about all of that as I began to draft my thank-you note to Bono (which was pretty cool in itself).

As I wrote, I thought a lot about when he said my words are like a punch. I hadn't ever really thought of my voice as something *powerful* before—only as something that came out when I opened my mouth. But Bono gave power and importance to my words, my opinions, my story. And it was like I suddenly had a new significance. A new purpose. I had been unintentionally searching for meaning behind my assault and my clubfoot, and now I felt like God had opened a door for me. Bono's words—which I truly believe were the voice of God coming through a rock star's mouth—had completely and fully kick-started my transformation. I now knew what I had to do: use my voice. I just didn't know how. Not yet.

Bono's prayer was also on my mind: "Make yourself available for work." I'd been so focused on the assault and trying to place it into my life and the plan *I* believed God had for me that I'd forgotten to include God and *His* plan. I wasn't searching for God in the midst of this crazy time in my life—and because I wasn't looking for Him, I wasn't allowing Him to come in and work in my life, and show me the next possible step in the Great and Amazing Plan He Has for Me. In other words, if my life, at that point, was a rock-climbing wall, I was so focused on where my feet already were that I wasn't looking up. I wasn't reaching for the next handhold. But not even that; I wasn't relying on the harness and rope at all. I was exerting so much energy holding on when I could just lean into the harness, fall away from the wall, and let the rope catch me.

I wanted to let God work in my life—I wanted to rely on God and let Him take control. I wanted to let Him work in me; it was only a matter of saying yes.

I started at Los Gatos High School in the fall—and only two weeks in, I knew that it was a better place emotionally for me than Canyon had been. At this point, it'd been three months since I met Bono—three months since I'd been challenged, changed, inspired—and I was aching to do something. *Anything*. To answer the call and make Bono proud. To prove that I could come out and make my mark not as a victim but as a survivor; and, more than that, a fighter. A warrior. Someone who could not only rebound but could *thrive*.

So I was thrilled (and incredibly nervous, a combination that was becoming a theme in my life) when, a few weeks after school started, Omaze visited our home to film a short documentary about my story. They interviewed me and my family and followed me to school, and it was weird. And uncomfortable. I never thought of myself as being someone other people would be interested in. And now, I had a camera following me to school. In between classes and everything. I was treated like some big, important person, but I was still just Chloe. I walked onto my school campus with a camera in front of and behind me, with a boom microphone attached to each camera, and people stopped . . . and stared. All of a sudden, I went from getting no attention at Canyon to everyone wanting to be my friend at Los Gatos. And a lot of the attention felt fake. Like I was trying out for an indie movie about some poor, disabled girl recovering from her assault, but all I was really doing was living out my day-to-day life on camera. And being followed and caught on film made me extra self-conscious about my school routines. For instance, I always walked alone to school. I didn't walk with anyone between classes. I never knew who to hang out with during break, so I always went to the art room to eat my snack and work on projects. I was still new and trying to figure out who I could be friends with. And it was all caught on camera. But the awkwardness of filming and everything that went along with it was, eventually, worth it. Since being completed, the documentary has been viewed and shared over 40,000 times. My story has been *heard* more than 40,000 times. Because I said yes.

I also had the opportunity to share my story on NPR's *Perspectives* radio show. After my episode, one person commented, quoting something I'd said: "The parts of us that society deems ugly, or weird, or abnormal need to be embraced and loved. We are each uniquely perfect, beautiful, and special." First of all, it was weird to be quoted. But then the listener continued: "These are truly great words of wisdom. You are an inspiration to me. I do not have any physical ailments, but on the inside I am an emotional mess full of wounds which have not healed. Thank you for the insight toward making me feel better about myself." I was starting to be *heard*. I was beginning to feel powerful. And because my words were helping others, I felt like I was doing something big and special and worth something. Because I was saying yes.

And it was only the beginning.

And remember, I'm not some incredible person who knows all the answers. It's hard to say yes. It was hard then, it's still hard now. And it might not ever get easier to say that small, three-letter word. But saying yes, from what I can see in just my own life so far, opens up doors and windows and all sorts of other metaphorical opportunities. I have no idea what I'm doing. Maybe I never will.

And maybe that's the point.

This whole concept of "faith" is just that: faith. Putting blind trust in something and someone that you want to believe in. And because I have faith in the God of Good Things, I have faith in His plan for me. And I demonstrate that faith by saying yes.

So *who knows* all the great things that could happen if we all say yes? How many authors, speakers, heroes, listeners, doctors, parents, friends, leaders could be born? Your yes is powerful.

Use that power. Say yes.

While I was brushing my teeth one night, getting ready for bed, I started thinking about what I would say, and how I would say it, if I had the opportunity to speak at schools. To share my message in the places it was needed most. And even though I'd always been quite shy, I began to get excited as I thought about possibly sharing with students. Though their stories would of course be different than mine, I knew there were others who were struggling in some of the ways I had. (And if you're one of those people, you're *not* alone. Ever. There are times for sadness, and there are times for kitchen dance parties. It's okay to be where you are right now. And when you're ready, I highly recommend a kitchen dance party to celebrate healing and God and *you*.) I wanted people like me to hear that what's imperfect in the eyes of the culture around us is actually beautiful in God's eyes. I wanted to inspire them to begin to see themselves as beautiful. And I also wanted them to hear about God's unique plan and purpose for each one of us. When I'd felt so invisible, it had been hard to see those truer-than-true facts. But as others began to receive my story, and even be changed by it, I'd started to see God's plan for me begin to unfold.

And I could do nothing but be confident that God would open the right doors.

CHAPTER 8

Heard

THE TRIAL WAS FINALLY HELD during the spring of my sophomore year in high school.

I did a whole lot of listening and feeling nauseous until April 11, when I was finally allowed to speak the truth on the stand. And I had *had* it. I was tired of sitting in the back of the courtroom (which is what I'd been doing up to that point), not being acknowledged as anything other than the victim, and listening to the perpetrators' parents complain about how court was taking too much of their daughters' study time and how the whole incident was just a "big misunderstanding." Even though I was SO READY to tell everyone how it really went down, I stressed about having to go on the stand. And since, on the first day I was testifying, I wasn't allowed to be in the courtroom until it was my turn (which felt dumb, because the accused minors—Cece and Allie—could listen to everything and hear everyone else testify before deciding if they wanted to get on the stand. What?! #victims), I'd just been hanging out in the victim's waiting room with my parents and the victims' services guy for three hours.

During this waiting time, I focused on what I'd done to prepare. I knew whatever I would say on the stand would be true, and I told myself that the facts would triumph. And since I was going to be sitting up in front of the court and the perpetrators and their families for who knows how long, and I'd want confidence, I had decided I needed to look cool. I'd worn a black shirt, a black leather skirt, black tights, and my black Converse high-tops (#edgy). Under my tights, my foot bore a fresh application of *beautiful*, and I'd also Sharpied the words *Strength in Brokenness* on my left forearm to remind myself that I could be strong. I was ready. I hoped.

But it was really hard. For weeks, I'd been sitting there, hearing those lies. Over and over and over again, listening to the defense attorneys make excuses for Allie and Cece, hearing about all the character witnesses called to the stand to talk about how Allie and Cece were "great girls" and would "never do something like this."

Though I wasn't in the courtroom at that time, my mom told me about Cece's and Allie's testimonies.

When the DA asked Cece why she'd written me an initial email to apologize, she said she was confused. That her mom and the principal and the police made her do it. When the DA asked Allie why she restrained me, she said it was because she was hugging me.

I had to remind myself that only the truth would triumph. *Only the truth will triumph.*

I never would have chosen a trial in juvenile court. It was very difficult on me and my family, and since they complained about it constantly, I can only guess it wasn't easy for Cece's and Allie's families either. But it's hard to say what would have been best for everyone. Early on, both Cece and Allie admitted they were guilty, in emails to me and to the school. But then something happened to twist that honest admission into a firm and consistent denial of what happened. Rather than guiding them to plead not guilty, I wish Cece's and Allie's parents or attorneys had given them the option, and equipped them, to continue to say, "Yeah, I did that. It wasn't cool. I do regret it. And I'm sorry." I think *that's* what could have helped us move on and heal.

During trial, I went on the stand and was questioned by defense attorneys for about an hour and a half. My DA had told me that I didn't have to look at the other attorneys if I didn't want to, and so that's what I chose to do. I listened carefully to what they were saying, but I didn't glance at them. At all. I answered their questions but never acknowledged the attorneys' physical presence. They were trying to find holes in my testimony—though there was only truth to be found. On the stand, *my* voice mattered. Only my voice. I could speak my truth and the judge could hear it, and that gave me power. And when I refused to look at those scheming defense attorneys, I used that power to honor myself.

My dad said it was epic. My mom said it was amazing.

But the defense attorneys were smart, and tried hard to somehow prove their clients were innocent. For instance, in my testimony, I'd said that the defendants had ripped off my shoes and socks. The video of the assault was played over and over, and the judge had *seen* what had happened. But Cece's defense attorney badgered me about whether the shoe had technically been "ripped" off, because he claimed that "ripping" would have been a swift, sudden act, and it actually took the defendant a minute or two to disrobe me, which obviously meant it couldn't have been a swift or sudden act.

Really?

As a result of this and similar attempts, by the end of the day, I was getting really tired. I'd been on the stand answering relentless, probing questions in front of the perpetrators, and I was ready to be done.

Allie's lawyer was wrapping up the interrogation when he paused dramatically to add, "Sorry, Your Honor, but there's one more thing . . ."

This was his big move. He posed it as an afterthought, but as he continued, it was clear that this is where he was planning to drive the nails into my coffin. He'd been planning this move since the very beginning.

He asked, "Chloe, is it true that you have a website promoting your story?"

"Yes," I answered proudly, still refusing to make eye contact with him.

No way could he possibly think I was anything *but* proud of Stand Beautiful and what it had become.

"And is it true that you sell T-shirts for profit?" he pressed.

"Yeah, I sell shirts," I confirmed.

"So it's true that you are using this incident for personal gain," he said, and I could imagine him raising his brow with the beginning of a sly smile.

"Sir, you cannot only make a statement. Please state your question, or your comment will be cut from the court transcript," the judge interjected.

With a dramatic flourish, the lawyer concluded, "No further questions, Your Honor." And he quickly sat down, smug. Actually, I wouldn't know how he sat down, because I never once looked at him, but I'm sure it was smug.

Poor guy thought he had me.

Then my DA interrupted, "It's okay, Chloe. Please tell the court what your website is about."

I looked over toward the judge, who nodded for me to continue.

"Well," I began, "after I was assaulted, I started my campaign, called Stand Beautiful. I didn't want anyone else to feel as alone as I did when they assaulted me."

The defense attorney quickly announced, "We've heard enough! Objection, irrelevancy!" This guy was so dramatic.

But the judge countered, "No, I want to hear her story."

She didn't even look at him.

My mom says that my whole body came to life when I was given the opportunity to talk about Stand Beautiful.

"I do sell T-shirts," I continued, "and the profits all go

toward organizations that value and enable transformation in people, whether it be physical, emotional, relational, or spiritual."

I noticed a smile on the judge's face.

I continued, "These people are broken, just like I was broken after my perpetrators assaulted me. So I want to support their journey and make sure, in whatever they're struggling with, that they don't feel as alone as I felt."

I was on fire.

The judge's smile grew bigger and bigger.

Out of the very corner of my eye, I could just barely see the defense attorney who'd brought it up continue to sink lower and lower in his chair until his suit was wrinkled, and he ceased to be relevant.

Sitting up there on the stand, speaking my truth, felt incredibly empowering. Sharing how Stand Beautiful was changing the lives of others, just because I was speaking honestly about my assault and healing and how we all need to embrace others regardless of their differences, made me realize that I was worth so much more than any of the drama that was unfolding in court.

And that was incredibly cool.

The trial had been all about sifting through evidence and testimony to find out the truth of what had happened. But during that time, I was also sorting out the truth about *me*. Would I ever be completely "normal"? While I saw my foot as beautiful, was there something so wrong with me, according to the rest of the world, that I deserved to be treated as a victim and only as a victim? Could there be more to me than just my clubfoot? As we were trying to prove to the court that I was different, that I had a disability, I was desperately needing and wanting to know that I really wasn't so different from everyone else. A pretty ironic contradiction, if you ask me.

But as I began to heal, I began to see that everyone has *something* going on. We all have a part of us that doesn't fit the narrow mold of what our culture has deemed "beautiful." One person doesn't like how her thighs touch. Another hates how hers don't. Someone else wants to be shorter or taller, or wishes they had a completely different body type. We *all* have something. And our temptation is to do everything we can to contort ourselves into the shape that others deem acceptable.

But as I got stronger, I began to see how stupid it was, wasting so much time trying to squeeze into society's mold. As I went to therapy, prayed, talked with my youth group leaders, and soaked up love from my parents and my brother, I decided that no one else got to decide if I was good enough. My bullies didn't get to decide. The girls gathered around them didn't get to decide. Victoria Secret catalogues and the girls on Instagram with seemingly perfect lives and bodies didn't get to decide. Choosing to believe that I was acceptable the way God had made me was *my* choice.

But it wasn't just some random feel-good thing I decided to believe about myself. No, my belief that I am fearfully and wonderfully made is rooted in the truth of what God says about us in Psalm 139:14. It's grounded in the reality that God's acceptance of me, through Jesus, is more real and true and solid than the opinions of others. Every day, I have the choice to either believe that I am God's beloved daughter, accepted as I am, or to believe that awful lie that says I'm not enough. I choose to embrace the truth that, despite my imperfections and challenges, I'm perfect because God made me just the way He wanted me to be. Entirely and fully beautiful. Entirely and fully His.

Day by day, slowly but surely putting one foot in front of the other, I am choosing to stand beautiful.

When it was time to return to the courthouse for sentencing, I felt empowered. Both my parents squeezed my hands once we returned to our familiar seats in the back of the room. And they wiped away their proud, happy tears. I felt like I had mighty defenders on my right and my left. These girls could never hurt me again.

Thoughtfully, carefully, the judge began, "I've spent a lot of time over the last few weeks considering everything I've heard. This was a very emotional trial, and I don't take it lightly. To some, Chloe's foot might be just a foot. But to her, it's much more than a foot."

Then she looked right at Cece.

"By doing this," she said, "you exposed something that she didn't want to expose."

The judge had understood. I felt like I could breathe again.

She continued, "As we've discussed, I can't find for the felony charges because no physical harm was done." I had suspected that going into the courtroom, since the official charge of 'hate-crime' didn't take emotional harm into account, but I continued to hold my breath for the final verdict. The judge finally said, "But I do take this incident very seriously, and find the defendants guilty of misdemeanor battery."

My parents and I reacted differently to the verdict. My parents were disappointed that the perpetrators were not found guilty of a felony hate crime, but were glad Cece and Allie were sentenced in the end. I understood why that was so important to them.

Me? I was pretty happy with what I got.

It meant that the judge had believed me.

It meant my body was worth respecting.

It meant that Cece and Allie had been held responsible for their actions.

It meant that my experience of being violated had been recognized.

And that was enough.

And for the first time since my assault, it finally felt right and authentic and good to forgive.

So I did.

CHAPTER 9

Barefoot AT THE NEW VIC

IN JANUARY, WE'D GONE TO a New Year's party at the home of some of my parents' friends. We were sitting out on the porch, and I started telling a friend of my dad's about my story. He explained that he and his wife facilitated the TEDx Talks in Santa Barbara. And that I should consider applying.

"Have you ever thought about doing a TED Talk?" he asked.

"Mmmm . . ." I weighed the possibility. Barely. "The thing is, I'm pretty shy. And I get super nervous talking in front of people."

"That's natural," he confirmed. "Just keep it in mind, though. Your story is a really interesting one. It's powerful. I think others would be interested."

Really? I knew my voice mattered to my family and people who loved me, but I didn't think that many "normal" people would be interested in what I had to say. TED and TEDx Talks were presentations done by experts who had deep insights on a topic, and audiences from around the world watched because they wanted to hear what that person had to say—that's a pretty big deal. I didn't think it made sense for me to give a talk like that. I was no one important or famous.

But the seed had been planted.

I again thought a lot about Bono and what he'd told me. "Pray that you'll be available for work, whatever that might be." I knew I had to speak about what'd happened to me, in some form or another. And even though it was *crazy*, I did a little research on TED as that Stand Beautiful message continued to form in my heart and mind. When I was supposed to be doing my homework, I filled out and submitted an application.

And I did so without telling my parents.

A month or two passed. I was in the middle of studying for finals when I got an email from TEDx Santa Barbara. They'd liked my application, and wanted a two-minute video of me speaking about Stand Beautiful. All I could think was, *I have to study, take finals, and pack for a two-week trip to Guatemala with church.* But with my dad's help, I made the video. And after I'd talked on camera for two minutes, attached it to an email, and clicked "send," I didn't give the video another thought.

I left for Guatemala (which was incredible, by the way), and I'd been there for eight days—without access to the Internet—when a kid from our group who somehow had Wi-Fi approached me with a funny look on his face.

"Hey, Chloe," he said, "I just got a text from your mom, and she said you need to check your email."

"Okay," I answered, confused. "Thanks."

"Oh, and Chloe? How'd your mom get my number? It's creepy, right?"

I laughed.

Once we were at a guesthouse in Antigua where we could finally get online, I discovered I had a ton of emails from TEDx. One of the most recent ones had been forwarded to my dad, with the subject line, "Good news, but we can't reach Chloe." I scanned the emails as quickly as I could. I'd been selected to give a TEDx Talk at the TEDx event in Santa Barbara. *I'd been selected.* But the event was in only six weeks. Which meant I had SIX WEEKS to write a whole eighteen-minute talk and completely memorize it. I was incredibly excited—and incredibly terrified. I'd never spoken in front of an audience before. And this talk was going to be *eighteen* minutes long. Without any notes or screen prompters. About my incredibly personal story. In front of three hundred people live, and thousands of people who'd be live streaming.

No pressure.

TEDx Santa Barbara hooked me up with an awesome speaking coach, who talked me through all my rounds of freak-outs and helped convince me that I was capable of doing this. She really understood how to connect with an audience and, knowing I'd be nervous, encouraged me to address just one person at a time, and then another, which would help make the audience feel not as big (which sounded great). She taught me to memorize one paragraph a day, and she encouraged me to be vulnerable. And to not be scared of getting emotional. Which I was scared of.

There was so much to memorize, and I was *so* nervous. Every time I'd think about it, my heart started beating faster and my chest felt like there was this huge weight on it.

I, for one, was not born ready to be a speaker. Even now, every time I have to get up before my class to give a presentation, I get nervous. And I'm sure you can relate. In whatever speeches you've had to give (whether it's your final English presentation, an award acceptance speech, valedictorian speech, your "I'm running for class office" speech, or even when you're just called on in class), I'm sure you've experienced at least a little nerves. And if you haven't, good for you. You have a natural talent I definitely don't have.

Thinking about giving this TEDx Talk, I had, like, 437 more fears than I usually do. I worried about everything that could go wrong. Because *so much* could go wrong.

I could forget everything.

I could cry the whole time.

My voice could shake like crazy throughout.

I could make a nervous joke and be really awkward.

I could pee.

Or fart really loud.

Or get so anxious from the nerves that I threw up.

Or get a tickle in my throat.

Or I could trip walking out onto the stage and faceplant, and break my nose.

Or my neck.

So many bad things could happen.

But I was also excited for the opportunity to share my story. This was what I'd been waiting for. It was the work for which I'd made myself available—and I felt so blessed that God had allowed this to happen.

I wanted to be ready. But I wasn't sure if I'd ever be.

Two weeks before my big speech, my dad got an email from a woman at (RED). Omaze had sent her the documentary they'd made about me, and also let her know about my upcoming TEDx Talk. Then she low-key told Bono about the talk, and he drew me a picture, which the woman emailed to my dad.

Let's just take a minute to process that. Because I still am. Bono heard I was nervous, and drew me something to make me feel better. What?! I still don't get how he's so cool.

Anyways.

My dad forwarded me the email, and when I saw it I freaked out (naturally).

In Sharpie, Bono had drawn quick, energetic strokes, depicting what looked like a female face—mine?—with chin-length hair, full lips, and scribbly eyes. He'd also written a message, which had been painted in a heavier ink line. It read:

Fellow comrade Chloe

Your head and heart are a perfect Rhyme

Behind the black-inked message was a heart, painted in cherry red.

And he'd signed it:

your fan, Bono

Your Fan? I was blown away. Bono had taken time from his busy rock-star life to create artwork for *me*. I couldn't believe it. I was amazed.

And more determined to do the work.

Unfortunately, Bono's reassuring words weren't enough to keep me from continuing my extended freak-out. A few days before my TEDx Talk, I suddenly felt the need to share all my doubts with everyone at the dinner table.

"Oh no. No, no, no, no, no, oh boy. I never should have applied! I'm gonna mess up and forget everything and no one's going to like it and it's all a mistake and I'm not ready for this!"

My parents, who'd seen my anxiety building, exchanged glances. They were used to my last-minute freak-outs. Everyone except for me understood that it was a reoccurring theme: I tended to doubt myself and my decision making (even though I'm probably one of the most careful decision-makers ever) before anything big happened. For example, I'd somewhat recently declared, "I shouldn't go to the party because I won't know anyone there," "I shouldn't go to Guatemala this year because my heart isn't ready," "I shouldn't go out with that guy because he might not be right for me," and "I shouldn't give a TEDx Talk because I'm not ready for this. I'm not prepared, they made a mistake." It was pretty predictable.

"But you *did* apply, and you *were* chosen!" my mom reminded me. "That's a really big deal."

And that's exactly why I was freaking out. It *was* a big deal. I'd heard my dad referencing different TED Talks for years. He's a designer—an innovator, a planner, a problem solver—and he'd always wanted to give one. I was nothing compared to that; just some teenager who'd been born with a messed-up foot who happened to walk into an assault. Those people who'd given TED Talks had spoken because they had it all figured out. I didn't even know what "it" was, but I was certain that I did *not* have that special something figured out.

"Chloe, you'll be fine! If I can do it, you can too. Duh." Tucker looked at me and made a silly face, and I smiled and made one back. Tucker's a gifted actor and musician, who plays the piano and drums and basically every other instrument, *and* can sing. The kid has no stage fright at all. I'm pretty jealous, actually. Not that I'd ever admit any of that to him, as his ego would get so big his head would explode.

It was easy for him to say I'd be fine because he is such a natural on stage. Me? No way.

"Well," I protested, "I knew I wanted to share my story in some way, but I think I went too big. Why didn't I start small?!"

Only God had the answer to that one.

And Tucker. Obviously.

My talk was on a Saturday. I'd started my junior year on Thursday, so when Tucker and I got out of school on Friday, we drove the four hours down to Santa Barbara, where my nanny and papa live. We brought along our closest family friend—and the closest thing I have to an older sister— Marianne, and my mom's sister, Auntie Kimmie. On the morning of my TEDx Talk, I was going to be surrounded by all of my favorite people. And that felt good.

The car ride to Santa Barbara was full of music, laughter, and jokes. I was sitting behind my dad, Marianne was in the middle, and Tucker was behind my mom. Marianne had to take an online class, so she was on her phone trying to work while Tucker and I (like the annoying, theoretical younger siblings we are) kept interrupting her with jokes and songs from *High School Musical*. I was anxious, and all that energy put me in a silly mood. Tucker, who is rather silly most of the time, was in his element. I think my mom and dad were just really, really nervous for me, as they didn't talk much.

My parents had been so incredibly supportive the whole

time since the assault. Heck, they'd been awesome parents my whole life. But I also know that they were still hurting from what had happened to me. Because, really, when those two girls assaulted me, they assaulted my entire family. All of us had been hurt by what had happened.

Tucker changed schools.

My mom cried more.

My dad spent hours on the computer writing emails.

And me? I shut down.

But that was about to change.

The venue for my TEDx Talk was a beautiful old theater called the "New Vic." The outside had pitched roofs and three sets of red wooden double doors, making it appear like an old English-style building, but the inside was completely redone. Seating three hundred, it looked like a small Broadway stage. But it didn't feel small. It all felt *big*.

During my rehearsal, the theater was empty except for my voice coach and my parents and some other speakers getting mic-checked. And some random people who wanted to watch the rehearsals because they didn't have tickets to the actual event. So, no, it actually wasn't empty. At all. It just wasn't as full as it could have been. As it was going to be the next day.

I thought I was going to throw up.

But I did it. I gave my whole speech during that practice session.

Without throwing up.

I was ready.

The night before the big event, TEDx held a pre-party for all of the speakers. There was an author, a musician, a business founder, a professional communicator, a psychologist, a successful entrepreneur, a CEO, an inspirational firefighter, a researcher, and a fashion designer. And me.

I quickly caught on—after a few awkward conversations—that the appropriate icebreaker was to ask what the other person would be speaking about the next day.

"The clarity of disruption."

"Power through insecurity."

"Rooftop leadership."

"Becoming fail-worthy."

"The rewards of not knowing."

"The missing link to your health."

And me.

"I feel totally out of my league," seemed to be an appropriate title for my talk.

As I worked my way through the appetizer table—because what else do you really do at a party full of adults during dinnertime where they only have wine (#underage) and appetizers?—I scrambled to think how I might identify myself to others at the party as someone who had a story worth hearing.

"My name's Chloe, and I'm disabled but it's okay" seemed too aggressive.

"Hi, I'm Chloe, and I was assaulted, but I met Bono, and

you'll hear about it tomorrow" seemed likely to confuse and traumatize people.

"Hey, I'm Chloe, and am sixteen and feel totally out of place, but why are you here?" seemed desperate and would most likely end in a long, awkward laugh on my end and a long drink of wine (#imstillunderage) on the other end.

I ended up going with something more along the lines of, "I started a movement called Stand Beautiful, which is all about loving and accepting our differences, after struggling with self-acceptance for so long. I'm sure you'll hear about it tomorrow, as I'm kicking off the day, but I'm excited to be here!"

It was good, if I do say so myself.

As someone who's not naturally energized by socializing with strangers (#introvertsletsgo), I was quite happy to climb back into my dad's SUV for the drive back to our condo and crash into bed. I slept like a baby. And my parents got no sleep at all, they were so nervous.

What they and I didn't know was that I was about to blow their socks off.

The day I gave my TEDx Talk, the third Saturday in August, two days into my junior year of high school, was arguably the best day of my life.

On the day of TEDx (!!), I woke up early, showered, and got dressed. The five of us—Dad, Mom, Tucker, Marianne, and I—left together at 6:45 a.m. Nanny and Papa and

Auntie would meet us there right before the whole thing started. We were all so excited! And nervous. And scared. And pumped!

Tuck, Marianne, and I squished into the backseat as my dad drove to the New Vic. We'd all put on the "beautiful" temporary tattoos we sell on my website, and, of course, took a selfie (#istandbeautiful). My mom turned on U2's "Invisible," and we listened to it on repeat, dancing and singing along for the fifteen minutes it took us to get there. Sitting in the backseat, with my favorite people, singing the best song ever, looking out the window as the sun rose over the palm trees on the beach, traveling to the destination where I knew my life would be changed . . . everything felt right. It's remained one of my best and most favorite memories. My dad was hitting all the high notes, my mom was looking over her shoulder smiling and laughing, Marianne was air-drumming, Tucker was dabbing, and I was taking it all in.

These were my people, this was my place, and it was my story. It was my time.

We arrived at the theater at seven, where my dad pulled open one of the heavy red doors and ushered me into the space I'd been preparing to inhabit every day for the last six weeks. When we walked through the lobby and into the theater, it was already set up with the TEDx backdrops, as well as the signature nine-foot-wide red circle on the stage that TED speakers always stand in. We headed toward the busiest-looking person with a clipboard and headset, who

welcomed us, gave us our nametags and lanyards, and ushered us backstage.

I couldn't believe it was real.

Even though I was so nervous that my foot wouldn't stop
bobbing as I sat in the downstairs backstage area, I consciously told my parents I was okay, that they should go
find seats and let me hang out back there. All I wanted to do
was curl up between them and let them whisper affirming
words, but I knew this was about me. Choosing to apply
and then give this talk had been the first big decision I'd
made on my own since choosing to go to Canyon freshman
year. And that meant I had to do this for myself. This was
my journey. They'd helped me get here, but I had to do this
part alone.

At 9:01 (because being right on time is tacky), a host
welcomed those who had filled every seat in the theater.
I was still sitting downstairs, doing about twelve different calming yoga breaths simultaneously and drinking
water to soothe my throat—but not too much so I didn't
live out my fears and pee on stage. I knew they'd come get
me any moment for my talk, and I was freaking out. (As I
always am.)

I was brought up the dark stairs, and was given the
clicker for my presentation as a young woman taped my mic
to my face. I remembered all of the pre-talk rituals I'd heard
of and that had been recommended, but instead of jumping

up and down or doing some yoga pose, I thanked God for getting me there, prayed that it'd go well and that He'd be heard through me, and then took some deep breaths. As the host finished up, I kicked off my suede Birkenstocks, slid them under a folding chair, and felt the cool floor under my feet. Nervous, but refusing to entertain thoughts of all the things that could go wrong, I closed my eyes and smiled to myself.

The host introduced me with the words, "Kicking off the day as our Keynote Speaker is sixteen-year-old Chloe Howard. Please give her a warm welcome. We're very proud of her." A kind older man with a headset gave me the thumbs-up and lifted the black side curtain for me to slide through, and I felt a surprising sense of calm as I walked through the blue lights and the see-through props, across the black stage toward that iconic red circle.

And I stood there. Taking it all in.

I looked out at the crowd. Heard the applause die down and found my people on the far-right edge of the audience. I looked at the timer on the dark back wall, set and ready for my eighteen minutes, and then looked down at my feet. *My* feet. Standing on that red circle. My beautifully scarred and discolored, toenail-less, naked feet on that red circle-shaped carpet. I saw my *beautiful* temporary tattoo on the outside of my foot, and I was proud. I looked up, took in a breath, and began my future.

"In the US alone, a student is bullied every ten seconds of every hour, of every day, three hundred and sixty-five days a year. And every single day, 160,000 kids skip school because they're bullied. That's over 187 million hours a year of fear. Pain. And hate. And those are just the incidents that are reported."

The longing I'd carried for almost two years, the deep desire to make meaning of my suffering, was satisfied in that moment, in those first fifty-six words. I felt strong. Powerful. Genuine.

"I know what being bullied feels like . . ."

As I began to share my story with 291 strangers, I felt a strange sense of peace. For the first time in a long time, I felt like *me*.

For seventeen minutes, I shared my truth, my beliefs, and the message that every person is worthy of dignity and respect and love.

At the end of my talk, I wanted to speak to the hearts of each person who'd gathered that day. I wanted each one—those without a physical disability and those with, those who'd never been bullied and those who had (and maybe even those who had been the bullies)—to leave understanding what it meant for *them* to stand beautiful.

"Accept your insecurities," I challenged the audience, "because we all have them. And you are each perfect in your own imperfect way. Love yourself. Because you deserve to be loved. Rock those differences! Embrace those imperfections. You are worth celebrating! I choose to stand beautiful before you today because my worth comes from within. And I know that I am someone worth celebrating. And so are you.

"Stand beautiful with me. Thank you."

As the audience applauded and stood up and cheered and cried and smiled, I paused to listen and savor the moment. This was *my* moment.

I returned backstage as the host welcomed the next speaker. I grabbed my Birks, got a couple high fives from the crew, and found a spot downstairs to sit down and wait until the break. My heart was thumping in my chest to make up for how calm I'd been up there, and I couldn't stop smiling. For twenty-one months, I felt like I'd been ignored, dismissed, minimized, and disrespected, first by the school I attended and then by defense attorneys. And this moment, of speaking what was most true for me, felt like a real gift. It didn't erase what I'd been through, but it was an opportunity to find meaning in it.

Other speakers and organizers came over to tell me I'd done a great job. I got texts from my friends and family and youth group leaders who'd been watching live online (and not that it's any more significant than everyone else's congratulatory texts, but the guy I liked had watched it live and texted me saying I did a great job and that it was awesome and, you know, that didn't hurt). At the intermission, I walked outside the theater to join my family. Members of the audience stopped me to express how brave I am and how I'd inspired them. My family ran at me with open arms; my mom had happy tears, my dad was laughing, Marianne was jumping up and down, Auntie flashed a thumbs-up, Papa patted me on the back and congratulated me for being awesome, Nanny talked about how good my outfit looked on stage, and Tucker told me that I was amazing and, by the way, he saw Vanessa Hudgens in the audience (which was true. And very random. #goals?). I was overcome with joy and pride, and was relieved it was over but sad to see it go. I never wanted to stop celebrating. I felt like I could do anything. And I wanted to do it all again.

I was heard and appreciated and loved. And I was able to inspire people.

I was more Chloe that day than I'd been in a long time.

For sixteen minutes and thirty-four seconds, I had proved, to myself and to others, that I was infinitely more powerful than what had happened to me.

We drove back to Los Gatos on Sunday afternoon. After dinner, I tried to finish the homework I'd put off while I'd been preparing for my talk, but all I could think about was every single second of the previous day. *Just* twenty-four hours ago. It felt stupid and irrelevant to waste time doing homework when I'd just given a *TEDx Talk*. I couldn't focus on my homework. I lay in bed staring out the window for hours, just living that day over and over again. I wasn't ready for it to be over.

Thinking about going back to school the next day was rough. "Let down" doesn't even begin to describe it. I'd just experienced this amazing high, and now I was being thrown back into the real world, where I was just regular Chloe. If I had my choice at that moment, I'd have been done with high school and out there spending my days changing the world. After my missions trip to Guatemala, and then preparing for two months to speak—and then actually speaking—I suddenly felt like I didn't have anything left to look forward to.

But I also knew there was so much more I could do. Many new speaking opportunities had opened up thanks to people in the Santa Barbara audience, and I could look forward to that. So even though I had to go back to school, I decided to focus on the positive. I mean, what other choice did I have?

Well, Monday at school turned out to be a giant mix of good and bad.

I left late for my walk to school, and got to my first period three minutes after the bell rang. Unfortunately, my history teacher locks the doors during class, so I had to knock and walk in all red-faced and sweaty after rushing to school. It was so uncomfortable. *I* was so uncomfortable.

I had Physics third period, and I really liked that class. I had friends in there, and our teacher was fun. After Physics, while I was walking to lunch, a bunch of people said hi to me, which felt good. I noticed that the same thing happened after school too. As I headed off campus for my walk home, I realized that a lot of people liked me; I was always so focused on how I was acting and walking and standing and talking—really, how others saw me in general—that I'd never actually noticed all the people who said hi before. And I realized I was already feeling a lot more confident than I had the previous year. I don't think that newfound assurance was all just because of my TEDx Talk, but it sure didn't hurt.

At youth group a couple Wednesdays later, we talked about self-worth. Everyone around the circle shared how they'd been feeling about their selves, and I'd been trying so hard to come up with a good answer that I hadn't noticed my turn quickly approaching. Which was why I was so surprised at how easily and quickly I responded.

I heard myself say, "I don't really have a lot of self-worth . . ."

As I kept saying more about struggling to believe that I was worth loving, internally I questioned whether what I was saying was actually true anymore. It definitely had been true my ninth-grade year, when typical teen insecurities were unfortunately confirmed, amplified, etcetera, etcetera. But I also realized that there were other times, like That One Time I Gave a TEDx Talk, when I felt amazing and powerful and unstoppable. So which was *more* true?

When youth group ended, two of my friends came up to me to reaffirm me and tell me that I was kind, and hilarious, and beautiful, and how it seemed like I had everything together. Still confused at my immediately negative response earlier, I awkwardly thanked them and left.

As I drove home from youth group, I weighed what they'd said. There were times when I had believed everything they'd described me as: nice and funny and pretty. Like when I was on stage. Or wearing my favorite shirt. Or meeting someone new in an environment I felt safe in, or even talking to that same guy I liked. But there were other times where I forgot I was no longer the victim. I'd lived as a victim for two whole years. I was used to not having confidence and used to being depressed about my life and myself. And I realized, in a quick moment, I'd jumped backward and identified myself as the victim all over again. Even though I thought I was past that.

And I wondered how I, Chloe Howard—the girl who somehow stood onstage for sixteen minutes and thirty-four seconds, talking about believing we are Beautiful and Worth It—could still somehow think of myself as the victim. Could still think of myself as worthless. As worth *less*.

As I parked in front of my house and sat in the dark car, I understood that each day I have the choice to live out the reality of my insane belovedness. And you have that choice too, because God says we're worth it. Because Jesus says He died for us. Because we are loved so completely and fully and created with *purpose*. We have a choice. We don't have to listen to the lies that say we aren't good enough. We don't have to play victim.

Every day you walk down the halls of your home or your school, you can choose whether you will listen to that lie—"You're ugly," "You're worthless," "You're invisible"—or whether you will choose to walk in the truth of "You're mine," "You're accepted," "You're loved."

I'm not saying it's easy. It's not. If anyone can testify that it's not easy, it'd be me. It takes courage. And I found myself hoping I had the courage to make that choice. To have the courage to not default to victim every time. To have the courage to choose to see the love. To believe the love and to believe the truth. Even on the days that just *suck*.

I'm sure you've had days like that, where the weight of life makes you feel like the choice has already been made for you. Days when it's really easy to believe those lies.

When you tell a boy you like him, and he says he might like you back, but then he changes his mind (true story).

When your best friend in elementary school dumps you for cooler friends in sixth grade (again, true story).

When your dad leaves home, and says it's not about you, but you feel like it really is (my friend's true story).

When you apply for an internship, or a college, or a scholarship, or a job, and the person who interviewed you says, "No." (I feel like we can all relate to this one.)

But when those around you—your parents, your friends, your boyfriend, your "we're just friends!", *whomever* it may be—say words or do things to make you feel small, you can choose to claim what is most true about you.

I had one of those days recently. Which involved too many of the things on that list. So I had to choose whether I would agree with the lies that say I'm not worth much, or whether I would listen to the truth that I *am*.

At the end of this pretty sucky day, I had to write to myself in my journal.

Chloe! You are awesome. And deserve to be with people who recognize that and want to be with you. Don't settle for anything less, do what makes you happy, and don't spend time with people who suck and make you feel inadequate or not 100 percent amazing. You're so. Incredibly. Cool. And fun. And beautiful. And special. And hilarious. Remember that!! Anyone that gets to spend time with you is incredibly lucky, Chloe! You are loved by so many people, so spend time with those people.

Remind yourself of that truth. And sure, laugh at me all you want for being the girl who has to give herself pep talks to remind her that she's worth it, but it's something I recommend. Whatever you can do to help you live in that truth. That you're special and one-of-a-kind and don't deserve people that treat you like that. Do it. Because if you want to believe that you're worth it, putting in the work to get there is too.

CHAPTER 10

THE BEGINNING OF *Now*

DURING THE SUMMER OF 2017, I had the amazing opportunity to partner with CURE International on a multi-country "Stand Beautiful Tour," where I would have the opportunity to share my story with thousands of people around the world. CURE's mission is to "heal the sick and proclaim the kingdom of God." The organization has hospitals and programs in twenty-nine countries, where they serve and treat and love on children with clubfoot and other deformities presenting at birth or later.

The minute my parents told me about CURE, I just *knew* that I had to be a part of it. Because the mission of CURE is to heal children both physically *and* spiritually. They take the lies told to these beautiful children—that they're cursed and that their parents are to blame for their disabilities—and completely rewrite those stories. CURE helps children relearn what it means to be truly loved, and teaches them that they are special because God made them with purpose. This story of transformation spoke to me. Because, in so many ways, it's my story.

But I didn't know what I was doing or even what I was walking into. I didn't have medical skills to offer; I was only sixteen. I didn't have millions of dollars to donate; I was only sixteen. I wasn't even old enough to join the summer trips for college students; *I was only sixteen.* But I just had this deep sense of knowing that this opportunity, whatever it might mean, had my name on it.

And then God showed up again.

It seems to be a reoccurring theme.

God made this trip happen, and within five months of first hearing about CURE, my mom and I had an itinerary and we were *going.*

And I was more excited about it than anything I've ever been excited about before.

But I was also nervous. Like before most big things that have happened in my life, I didn't feel ready. While I'd heard great things about CURE, I hadn't seen the organization in action yet. And because I've been hurt by the Christian world—places like Canyon Christian, where adults didn't protect me and often used Jesus as an excuse for their actions—I began to worry that maybe CURE was just an international, medically-based Canyon. Would the people at CURE really do what they said they would do? Would they really show up and care for *any* child? Would my heart be ready to be open to believing that good things can come out of a Christian organization? I was so hoping that I would find truth at CURE.

And I did.

Our trip with CURE was broken up into sections: our time in Pennsylvania at the headquarters for training and preparation, then to the Dominican Republic, Kenya, and finally India to do the work we'd signed up for. At each of the three international destinations, I was going to spend time in hospitals with the children who had clubfeet, talk to families, patients, and staff, and just love on the people and demonstrate what it means to stand beautiful. While I'd spoken about my foot, the assault, and about Jesus with many people by this point, I was worried about how people who also had clubfeet would respond. What if they didn't appreciate what I had to say about my own clubfoot journey, or thought I just didn't understand true pain because I was a white girl of privilege?

I tried to push those thoughts aside during that first week at the Mission Support Center in Pennsylvania. There, I heard stories of how CURE is *actually* doing what they say in their mission statement. They show up, pray, care for, and show love to the children, families, and caregivers in their hospitals and clinics all over the globe. Over and over, I heard stories of how those working with CURE have made a difference in the lives of children who many people in this broken world think of as throwaways.

The babies born underweight and with disabilities who have no rights in Afghanistan.

Or the children that have been tossed out of their villages in Africa because their bowed legs don't allow them to walk, much less help their family to survive.

These children have thought of themselves as cursed and not worth anything. But CURE goes in and tells them Jesus sees them as an amazing gift to the world. That He has come for children like them—for children like me.

I was reminded that I'm a gift because of who I was created to be. (As are you.)

And with that in mind, I felt ready to go into the world and share that gift with others, and trust my words would be used to make a difference.

My mom and I arrived at our first location, the Dominican Republic, all too soon. There was no turning back. Standing there in that hot and muggy airport with our three massive suitcases and watching, hearing, and smelling the Latin culture surround us on all sides, I instantly began to have the same worries I'd struggled with at the training center. Here, people expected me to be this perfect, has-it-all-together speaker. That's what CURE had told them—that I was a speaker who'd traveled to share my personal clubfoot experiences and inspire them to love themselves. But the task was a lot to take in. Now, it was *real*.

Don't get me wrong, I wanted to do what Bono challenged

me to do—to let the work wash over me. To be available and ready for change. To let *myself* be inspired, moved, and changed, instead of focusing so much on the inspiring I felt I had to do. But it was me, the worrier who never feels ready for anything.

However, God was ready for me.

God began making His plan for the trip clear almost right away. Everything in Santo Domingo happens fast: traffic, food, conversations, introductions, procedures, meetings, surgeries—and life in general. And, realizing this, I became instantly worried (on top of the worries I already had) that our crazy-fast schedule would not allow time to slow down. To process.

Thankfully, God knew just what I needed.

My first international speech was the morning after we landed in Santo Domingo. One of the CURE employees acting as our designated in-country host had arranged for me to speak to their church's high school youth group, and I had practiced my talk and knew exactly what I was going to say and when. I had my notes printed and my presentation arranged and my Omaze documentary pulled up, all set to click play. Everything was precisely as it should be.

Except things didn't happen as I had thought they would. I was told I would speak to twenty or thirty students, but ten showed up. And I did not stand in front of an audience as I usually do—we sat in a circle of plastic folding chairs. Plus, I had forgotten about the whole translator aspect, which I was concerned (of course) would make my presentation longer and cause people to get bored. The video had to be translated, so it was paused every thirty seconds. My talk had to be interpreted, so I ended up just speaking and sharing instead of reciting and giving. And the whole language barrier thing was confusing on my end too, which made the Q and A section a bit long.

But it was perfect.

And I loved every single minute of it.

The students cried during my video. Smiled at me and applauded when it was over. It surprised me that, even with the video being repeatedly paused, they were still impacted.

And since I didn't refer to my printed-out talk at all, I simply told my story. Talked about my life. Honestly, I don't know a lot of what I said, because I don't think a lot of it was *me* finding those words. The kids were crying, the pastors were crying, my mom was crying. I got responses like "Life changing" and "So inspiring" and "I want to tell everyone at my school." (But said in Spanish. #stillinthedominicanrepublic)

I alone can't illicit those responses. Everyone crying, laughing, and thankful; I can't do that. I don't singlehandedly have the power to. But it happened.

Because God was in that room, pure and simple.

I had been so worried about not being ready or messing up or completely blowing the whole Stand Beautiful/ CURE partnership on the first day of the international tour.

I was worried about letting everyone down. About missing things. About not being ready for this trip.

And God knew that. So He showed up. On that first day. In front of that youth group.

And that's when I knew that it didn't matter if I was ready.

Because the truth is, we can't do it. We really can't. We can try our best and do what we think is the right thing, but in reality, none of us are capable of ever "doing it." Of being ready on our own. But that's actually okay, because it's not the way *we* show up that matters. It never has been. It's about God and how He shows up in us. Through us. And God can only make an appearance through us if we make ourselves available to Him. If we open up our hearts.

Later in the trip, I was standing in front of a crowd of maybe thirty hot and sweaty people gathered in a waiting room at the CURE Dominican Republic hospital. All their eyes were on me, and I didn't know what to say. So I did what I do best; I took time to think.

I looked down at those feet. *My feet.* Reddish, bluish, in places simultaneously fully both colors. Those ankles. Smallish, purplish. Different widths. Those toes. *My* little toes. Naked. Pointy.

Everything seemed just too small. Too narrow, too pointed, too greenish (there was definitely green in there too). Everything looked so *different* from a typical foot.

Scars: visible. Toenails: missing. Heel: bulbous. Foot: throbbing.

When I looked up, there were eyes. Lots of them. Brown. *Dark* brown eyes. Thick eyebrows. Coarse dark hair. And then, little hands. Reaching. Grabbing. Pointing. Picking. Digging. And little exposed feet. Curled toes. Dusty heels. Thick brown ankles.

Curved feet. Twisted feet. *Clubbed* feet.

Now, I remembered why I was there.

These people knew me. These people understood. They are like me and they are for me. We are connected. I realized all I needed to do was tell them my version of our shared story.

"Hola. Me llamo Chloe, y tengo diecisiete años. Nací con un pie equinovaro."

"Hello. My name is Chloe, and I'm seventeen years old. I was born with a clubfoot."

Just like them.

Once I'd focused myself, I proceeded to give my talk in the middle of that big clinic room. After I finished speaking, I told the audience of parents they could ask questions, expecting to make those connections ... but nothing happened. *Nothing.* I watched. I waited. Tentative arms patted restless babies, scratched heads. I looked out at the people gathered, watching and listening back. The moment felt like it lasted forever as I waited, repositioned my feet, smiled at four children. Then another one in the back. Still, no hands raised, not even to make a comment. No one made a sound. As I was beginning to doubt the feeling of certainty I'd had earlier, I heard a voice.

It was old. Careful, concerned, loud, and a bit raspy. I located her in the last chair on the left, with a tiny boy next to her. This boy was held so tightly against her that the woman's protruding figure and overall presence seemed to absorb him, and his little hands held tightly to her sweater.

"The mother isn't here. It's just me. The aunt. He's on his fifth round of casting, and his foot is getting better, but we think he might have something more. Something worse. I'm worried for him. Scared for his future, because *look at him.* He's different. How do I protect him? What can I do? What's your advice for me? What would you say?"

The translator looked at me apologetically. He knew it was a hard question; I knew it was a hard question. I gazed at the young boy sitting on the woman's lap, and I couldn't find an answer. I heard my mom, who was next to me, make a sound like she was about to speak.

I interrupted her.

I still didn't have any words. In fact, I had absolutely nothing to say. But in the end, I didn't *need* to have any words.

"I don't know the future. I can't tell you what's going to happen to this boy tomorrow or next week or in a year or in ten. And that's scary. But I know a God and love a God and trust a God who *does* know. Who knows tomorrow and next week and next year and the next ten. I'm not going to tell you that everything's going to be fine and that this young boy will never suffer, because I don't know that. But God knows. And He's got you. He *has* you. So we don't have to waste any time worrying about tomorrow. We just have to trust that God has a plan and a reason for *all* of this. I believe He does. And I think you want to believe that too."

All the people gathered in that clinic room smiled, then clapped. They wiped their tears and kissed their babies and held their heads high. In that moment, the fear in that room disappeared. There was joy. There was hope. And there was that shared experience I'd hoped for.

I smiled too, and wiped a tear and laughed and exhaled, because I knew that those words hadn't been mine.

This experience is one that stood out to me most throughout the trip, because I was so obviously unprepared, and God so clearly was present and swooped in. I believe the message He gave me was not just for that lady but for me too. God knew that I needed reminding that I don't need to worry—ever. I don't need to be scared—ever. All I need to do is trust that God will get me through all the doubt and worry and fear because He never leaves me. (And in case you're wondering, He's never going to leave you, either.)

We've established that I don't have the answers—that I'm not an expert in life, I don't have it all figured out, etc. ... but I know for a fact that God is always there for us, and He gives us what we need. I'm not saying that when we say, "Oh my GOSH, I *need* that [insert name of thing you don't actually need]," God gives it to us. God is Big and Powerful and All-Knowing and All-Loving, but God is not a magic prize machine. And there are times when we really, really want something to happen, but it's just not what God has planned for us at that time.

I have to remind myself that God's timing is perfect. In that moment, I *needed* God to show up. I *needed* Him to tell me in some way, shape, or form that He was there and would keep being there. Because God knew that *that's* what I most truly needed, He delivered.

And God's always going to deliver. It might not always be on our time, or be exactly what we expect, but He will.

The experiences I continued to have in the Dominican Republic were amazing, but, honestly, they began to feel overwhelming. And I was feeling that sense of exhaustion from dealing with the hugeness of everything when, on an incredibly humid day, with my stomach turning and twisting from some unkind food we ate the night before, we drove through the chaotic Santo Domingo traffic to the home of a girl my age named Guadalupe. And to tell the truth, I didn't really want to go. And with my hesitation, the old doubts started to creep back in. I questioned how this girl would ever be able to relate to me. She lives in a different world, with a different life story, speaking a different language. Would she even want to hear my story? What could I possibly say to her that she would care about? I had no idea.

Hers is a sad story. And a pretty crazy one. She was a typical fifteen-year-old girl walking home from the market one day, until, while on a bridge, a bus's breaks gave out and the vehicle ended up hitting her. The motion and force of the collision pushed her off the bridge, and she fell to the street below, where she was then run over by a car. Crazy. Miraculously, she didn't die or experience any sort of brain damage. She did, however, break her pelvis and shatter the bones in her leg, which led to many visits to the public hospital.

Most people in Santo Domingo know that the public hospital isn't great, and Guadalupe had a terrible experience. Her leg wasn't operated on properly, and it got infected. But unlike most people, she somehow found a CURE doctor, who saw her and came up with a solution that will, eventually, heal her completely.

I heard about Guadalupe's story from our CURE host during the drive to her house. And I wondered how it would feel to have *me* connect with her as someone who could relate. I mean, she was completely normal before the accident. And I've always been this way; I've had my little foot since I was born. It didn't seem like we'd have much in common. Especially as what she'd experienced seemed way worse than anything I've ever gone through.

And that got me thinking about how I interact with people in my own town. I have had people in my life say that I can't possibly understand the crazy stuff they have been through.

"You only have a clubfoot," they say.

What. Are. You. Talking. About. Really?

"You totally don't get my boy stuff/crazy mom/struggles with school . . ."

Huh? But I have problems too. Why can't you see that?

And in those moments, I have thought that maybe they were right. Maybe their pain *is* more real than mine. Maybe I have overplayed and inflated the physical and emotional pain I've been through. Maybe their breakups are truly more painful than my bone fusion. Maybe their best friend fights are worse than my assault. And I shut down, again, and feel guilty that I somehow "don't understand the real world" (as a "friend" once told me). My pain wasn't the normal kind—and maybe that meant it didn't matter as much in this normal world.

But then I remembered that God tells me that He sees my pain. And that it *is* real. And that it sucks. That I *have* been really, really hurt. But He promises me that He loves me and will heal that pain. And I believe Him.

And He sees and can heal *all* pain—there are no "normal" or "not-normal" levels in His mind, or judgments on the emotional and physical issues we deal with, so there shouldn't be in ours, either.

But because we as humans have a hard time understanding other people's experiences sometimes, God gives us the power to be empathetic—to be able to feel for someone else and their pain even if we come from completely different situations and completely different backgrounds. And so I began to feel confident that, even though I didn't fall off a bridge and get run over by a car, even though Guadalupe got to experience bodily freedom before her accident and I never have, even though our home environments are so incredibly different that they're not even worth comparing, we had something in common: a love for Jesus. And that love enabled us—me and Guadalupe—to feel for each other. To have empathy in light of our differences.

I had this in mind as I quietly entered this girl's family home and found an incredibly happy eighteen-year-old. Her mother welcomed us in and we sat, side by side, sharing our lives. I told her my story, and she told me hers. We shared our pain—and our loneliness—together. She'd felt ashamed of certain parts of herself, and so had I. She had hurt in her life, and so had I. She has a family that loves her, and so do I. She believes that Jesus will be with her, and so do I. And we shared reassurances and truths together.

As I sat there, in the heat, connected by pain and sadness, despair and repair, I started to think about the truth that we are all connected. I mean, the list of things Guadalupe and I *didn't* have in common went on for miles. But all that mattered, in that moment—sitting in the heat of the afternoon on that dusty zebra-print couch, waving away flies and listening to the dogs barking and the little naked children's feet pounding on the dirt road outside—was the knowledge Guadalupe and I were similar in more ways than one. No matter how different we may appear.

The Dominican Republic was my first experience in recognizing that I can *use* my foot. That it can give people hope for something they didn't know could have a happy ending. God was making it clear that sometimes the good things He plans for us don't even compare to the things we thought would happen. Despite all my worries and feeling completely unprepared (as usual), I was able to stand beautiful just by letting go of my life as I saw it, and letting God swoop in to catch me.

Every single person on this crazy big earth has something in their lives they were given for a reason but have no idea what to do with. And every single person on this crazy big earth can let go for a moment and let God take control of that one thing.

Trust me, He can do something really cool with it.

CHAPTER 11

Standing Beautiful

ALL OVER THE PLACE

KENYA IS A BEAUTIFUL COUNTRY filled with green mountains, thick, heavy fog, warm valleys, wild animals, crazy Nairobi traffic, and pot holes the size of swimming pools. Struggling to become more than an emerging country, Kenya is stuck with corrupt elections, gentle people, and the most perfect, light-up-an-entire-room little baby smiles in the world.

I was the most excited to travel to Africa because, just a few weeks prior, my family and I had the opportunity to see *The Lion King* on Broadway while we were in New York. Tucker and I were amazed by the rhythmic drums, and Mom and Dad kept smiling and laughing. We left the theater singing "Hakuna Matata"—with Tucker swinging his hips and belting out showtunes in the middle of

Times Square. If Tucker could have come with us to Africa, I think he might have put on the biggest song-and-dance celebration of all time.

Africa. *Africa*. All of it excited and scared me at the same time. When my mom and I exited the airport after a grueling twenty-five-hour day of flying, landing, and taking off over and over again, we were met with a hundred pairs of eyes. And looking around, our pale skin was incredibly different. We stuck out almost as much as I felt we did. It was almost midnight, we couldn't find our driver, and we didn't have cell coverage. For a few moments, we were stuck with tons of luggage, and no sense of what to do. But then my mom spotted our name being held by a very short Kenyan woman, and my heart skipped. We were going to be fine. I hoped.

I loved Martha from the moment I spotted her thin frame in that last little bed by the window in the CURE Kijabi hospital. Her eight-year-old face beamed in entirety at me as she raised her tiny, misshapen hand to wave—which really looked more like flapping, since she doesn't have any muscle tone in her arm or hands. Her big, brown eyes grew bigger as I walked over, and I couldn't help but reach down and hold her small hand in mine. She was *pure joy*. All she wanted to do was hold my hand and smile at me. Here we were, Chloe and Martha, two girls separated by continents, language, skin color, age, everything—but now together, sharing a smile. My smile told her that she was loved; and her smile back affirmed anything and everything.

While I'd met a lot of grinning children in the Dominican Republic, this interaction really struck me, because it showed she already knew she was accepted just the way she was—despite her clubbed feet and hands that don't work, or a body that is sick and might never get better. I saw her for all the beauty that is *Martha.* And in that moment, I also saw how God sees me. All the beauty that I am—even in my imperfect state. And I was overwhelmed with thankfulness and joy. Because Martha, who seems to have nothing, was so full of joy that it couldn't be contained. It *wouldn't* be contained.

I think about Martha a lot. And I think about how she finds that joy. How she *chooses* joy. And how I don't always carry that joy around with me. At home, I revert to the shy version of me—or the sarcastic version of me, or every other possible version of me that isn't truly fully *me*—leaving my real self buried just a little. I tend to wrap myself up in a bubble wrap wall of protection because I still have this lingering feeling that at any moment, something bad can happen again, and I need to be prepared. And this is where Martha's smile seeps in. What if I can be the real Chloe with my friends? Even with those who have hurt me? What if I stand beautiful in my own school, where the race for popularity, for being the prettiest/smartest/coolest is always in play? And what if I don't let it bother me? With a joy like Martha's, it wouldn't have to.

I was asked to a school dance last fall by a guy I didn't really know. But I was thrilled with the idea that someone asked me, so I said yes. Obviously. I got a dress I felt good in. I was excited to have an actual high school experience, because while I'd gone to dances, I had never been *asked*. For the first time, I felt chosen in a way I'd never experienced—even if it was by some guy I had no connection with. But then, a week and a half after showing up in my driveway with a "Praying you'll go to homecoming with me" poster at seven in the morning, he let me know that he didn't really want to go with me. There was this other girl he really wanted to go with, and she was suddenly available, and well, I'd understand. Or, he thought I'd understand. Especially if he took me out to the local coffee shop first. And *then* asked if I'd let him take the other girl. (#imnotyourmother)

"You are okay with it, right?" he asked over tea.

Ummm. Yeah. No. This isn't okay. It's really rude. And super embarrassing and awkward. Not cool.

Not only had he told our shared friends we were going to the dance together, he'd sent them a *picture* of him asking me. So they'd know something had happened when I wasn't the one he actually took.

"Oh, yeah. Sure. I get it." In the moment, I didn't know what else to say.

I was really annoyed when I got home, though. And even more annoyed that it bothered me so much. To the point of tears. I hadn't even really wanted to go with him, because I barely knew him. But I had wanted to *go*. And in this moment of insecurity and doubt and overwhelming *annoyance* with the teenage world, I figured I must not have whatever it takes to be a normal high school girl. I mean, a boy *unasked me*. That only happens in comedies to the funny-but-awkward, secretly beautiful protagonist. And it only happens in the plotline right before the nice, funny, attractive guy is revealed and says he's liked her from the back of the room for his entire life and will she please make him the happiest guy in the history of the world and go with him to the dance. And here's the thing: I hoped I was funny, and I knew for sure I was awkward. But I also knew there was no guy secretly in love with me; I tend to pick up on these things. How in the world was I ever going to get asked to a dance, be someone's girlfriend (I'm fun. I think I'd make a pretty excellent girlfriend), and get someone to marry me if I was so *nothing* that I was *unasked* from a stupid high school dance? Come on. Really?

When I get caught up in those types of feelings, I again think about Martha. She can't even walk. She can't even hold a crayon to color. But her smile? It was contagious. As I focus on those things, I realize once again that there is no one on earth (okay, maybe your mom or dad or brother or dog, because dogs are the best, and what did we do to deserve them) that can make you feel 100 percent worthy. The only real worth comes from Jesus. He's the only one who can provide pure, real joy.

I ended up asking a good guy friend of mine—someone

who totally gets me—to go to the dance with me. He planned a surprise limo ride and a fun pre-dance dinner (bocce ball and pizza. Pretty freaking awesome.), and we went with one of my best friends and her date too; as the night went on, I recognized that maybe it was supposed to happen this way. That I had to go through being asked and unasked if it meant having an even better time with my friends. I might have been one boy's throwaway, but I was another's prize. And that's how it is loving Jesus. I am His prize—and so are you. He says we're completely and fully 100 percent worth it. And that's a reality I can live with.

Meeting Martha wasn't the only experience that changed me.

When I got up on the chapel stage to speak to the staff at the CURE Kijabi Hospital, I could only focus on how incredibly nauseous I was (#itsafrica) (#dontdrinkthewater) (#ohno), and literally thought I was going to diarrhea myself. But once I said, *"Jambo, jina langu ni Chloe, na nilizaliwa na clubfoot"* ("Hello, my name is Chloe, and I was born with a clubfoot"), the nausea fell away, and without really preparing to do so, I was suddenly saying big and meaningful things. And for the second time, I knew that God was using my voice (because I am pretty much incapable of saying anything big or meaningful without any God help).

As I walked off stage, a lady seated behind me—one of the janitors—patted me on the back and shook my hand

and thanked me for reminding her that she makes a difference. A surgeon said the same thing, as well as several
nurses, two men who work in the workshop making braces,
a woman who works in human resources, and the spiritual
director. I quickly realized the message that needed to be
heard that morning was that they—all two hundred members of the CURE staff—are important. And so valued. And
that they are *all made* for this. Chosen by God to be right
there at CURE right then.

All of them, collectively, are changing the world for
these kids through what they do. It doesn't matter that some
are surgeons and some are the IT guys, because they are
all doing something *big*: they are all helping spread Jesus's
love. By being there and working for CURE, they have said
yes to God's plan in their lives; *that's* standing beautiful.

I felt like all of a sudden, the Stand Beautiful message
was out of my control—and I loved it. It was growing. And
it wasn't about my story anymore; it was, and is, about
everyone else's. It is about saying yes in all aspects: to God,
to yourself, to others, and to your body.

The clinic also showed me how important it is to say
yes every day, and not forget we *are* making a difference,
even when we don't see that difference right away, or when
things are difficult and we aren't sure we can do it anymore. I've been told life is about choices, and it seems like
standing beautiful is the choice to keep going. To tell yourself you are worth more, even on those days and weeks
where it feels like the entire world disagrees with you. To

treat others the same way you treat yourself, especially the people who are difficult to love. And to do whatever God calls you to do, from a small action at your school to a journey into the scary unknown.

I know, at least for me, that choice is a hard one. My life and the way I treat myself isn't going to change overnight. But I choose to stand beautiful and then *work* my way there. I don't know what my future holds—I hope to keep traveling, meeting new people, and sharing my story and all that—but no matter what is next, I want to continue to say yes to the opportunities I'm given, and stay open to whatever God has planned next.

I'm just saying yes.

After my talk, I had the opportunity to see another side of standing beautiful when I met this guy in his twenties named James, who'd been hired as a construction worker at CURE. I quickly learned that he's pretty cool. Especially since he shared something with me he doesn't often tell others.

When James heard about my staff talk in the hospital's chapel, and that I have a clubfoot, he immediately asked if he could meet me so he could share his story. The spiritual director at CURE Kijabi—who we spent a lot of time with—has known James since childhood. Which was why James's intentions for his meeting with me shocked him so much: James also had a clubfoot. And the spiritual director had no idea.

James and I sat down on a park bench in the hospital courtyard, and before we'd said much, he took off his shoe. So I took off mine. And just like people exchange numbers, we shared foot glances and scar viewings and treatment stories. I asked him why he didn't share his clubfoot with many people, and he told me about the reactions people had to his foot. And about all the problems it caused him and his family. I then understood that, even though we both have a clubfoot, we were different. And it broke my heart.

James said that when he was born, his dad left his mom because the man couldn't and wouldn't be in association with a deformed child. James said that it tore his family apart and wrecked his mother, but because she loved James, she devoted all her time and energy after the separation toward the clubfoot treatment. He talked about stigmas and how unfair they are, and how wrong it was that his dad not only left upon his birth, but returned and expected acceptance once James's treatment was finished.

And I didn't get it. How could I live in a world where James and I have the same deformity, but my dad loves me even more for it while his dad refused to be associated with a clubfooted child? How could I survive in this world having learned that, while what I went through was significant, what James experienced was even harder? How was that even fair?

But then I started thinking about Guadalupe again; how we had more in common than I initially thought. So, like I'd done two weeks earlier with her, I internally began listing the things James and I had in common: a clubfoot, surgeries, bullying. Guilt. James and I both dealt a lot with shame; him, when his dad left, because he felt like it was his fault. Me, after I was assaulted. We both had experienced unfair circumstances. And that, strangely, made it seem better—that James and I, though going through different experiences, were now talking through it together.

James seemed content after telling me his story and hearing mine, and while I was happy to have met him and gotten to speak with him, as he got up to leave all I could think about was the importance of standing beautiful. And how, when James was little, he needed to hear that he was not a mistake. That his clubfoot was not a curse. That it wasn't his fault that his father left.

I thought about James's mom. How important it would've been for her to hear that she did nothing wrong. That her child was beautiful and special, and that she was not at fault. That she demonstrated how good of a mother she is and how much love and determination she had by following through with James's treatment.

But I thought the most about James's father. How broken he must have been. How, for some reason, he and thousands of other spouses and siblings and family members leave these disabled children who need nothing *but* love. I thought about how things would have been different if he could stand beautiful.

And these thoughts only confirmed what I was learning each day:

Everyone needed to know the message. Of love and acceptance and determination and hope and joy and peace. Everyone needs to stand beautiful for others.

I'd originally thought that the Dominican Republic and Kenya were challenging, but India was on a whole new *level* of crazy-fun chaos. I'm not going to lie, I was anxious about going to India. Pretty much everyone—from friends, my doctor, my papa, even a random cab driver on the street in Dubai—told me to be very careful of the water, the food, the beggars. "You could get very sick," they said. "It could wreck your trip." So, yeah, I was anxious. And, I was one month into our journey. A whole month of being away from family, friends, my bed, my room, my brother, my dad, my two silly dogs. And I was tired. Like, exhausted. I guess being gone for so long will do that to you. So, walking out into the heat and humidity of Delhi that first night, right after landing, did not make me excited about being in the "land of dreams" (as I read on a giant airport poster). I believed that I'd seen everything there was to see of the world, and that I was ready to go home.

But there was still more I had to do. Still more I was *meant* to do. I wasn't done yet. In fact, I found out I was just getting started.

I was here—whether I wanted to be or not. It got me thinking about how many days in the past year, as I walked to school, I'd call my papa with the pretense of waking him up (he's retired now, and I love that I'm his alarm clock) when, really, it was because I needed someone to tell me that they love me, and that I'd be fine and would have a good day. I really don't have a choice about going to high school. But many days I find myself wishing that I didn't have to go—didn't have to face the fact that I don't have hundreds of friends, or, really, a place that I feel safe. So I call my pops and he, in his own quirky way, reminds me that I am great and worthy of love, and that gets me through another day. Being in India felt like that. Like I didn't really know if I wanted to be there, and that I needed my papa's encouragement to get me through this final leg of our trip. But instead of being able to call him, *I* had to remember why I was here, and I had to believe my own message. I had to stand beautiful in all my exhaustion and anxiety (#dontdrinkthewater), and acknowledge that Jesus would show up. As He tends to do.

When I saw my first Indian clubfoot clinic, I immediately knew why I'd needed to be in India. We traveled to many different clinics during our time in Delhi, but the first one stands out because it was our *first one* in India. And to tell the truth, Mom and I were a bit shocked. We walked into this public hospital in the middle of the city, and it just wasn't clean; there were so many people, and not enough room for them all. People were lying on the floor every-where, eating and sleeping and just waiting, and there was discarded trash and overflowing toilets. I've never seen as many people gathered in the same small place as I did in those hospitals. But the people were *lovely*. And this seemed to be a reoccurring theme. Beautiful people, finding community in their brokenness. That's what these clinics were like.

And it made me think. Here I am, living in rich America, where most people have almost everything they need—clean hospitals, running water, a toilet with a seat (!) and toilet paper every time. But on the inside, so many people are hurting. I can think of friends who put on that special smile at school because *God forbid* we're seen as the damaged, broken people we are. I can think of times *I* was hurting and tried to put on that smile—or tried to cover my pain up by clinging to whoever I could find, making bad jokes to get laughs, or making myself so available to guys that the rejection hurt even worse. We have *so much* but are lacking even more. And in India—where the need is material—the people don't pretend. They don't hide their hurt. They don't cover up their situation with bad jokes and even worse friends. Through their actions alone, I saw them for the honest people that they were. And I wonder if we could do that—look at the good and the bad honestly. What if we could all stand beautiful for what is good *and* right?

The CURE clubfoot clinics at the crazy public hospitals in India are pretty dang special. There are rooms and rooms of massive crowds of parents who hold their children for hours, waiting for the doctors' eyes. But these parents are safe here, and they know it. They have community even in the lonely isolation of having a child with disabilities. Because they have each other.

And these doctors care about them and their children. When asked what keeps them going on the busy days when their clinic alone gets two hundred patients, the doctors simply say, "I love these kids. I care about them, and I'm invested in their treatment. I do it for them. And when you love what you do and who you do it for, it's not work."

I remember walking into a clinic room and immediately being surrounded by fifty parents and children all pushing to get a glimpse from Dr. Matthews. He is a surgeon at St. Stephen's Hospital, and watching him work was amazing. He was like happiness with legs. He was oldish and shortish, and joy erupted from his mouth and eyes and fingertips. He had a big ear-to-ear grin all the time, and his eyes legit twinkled. He's known throughout India as a saint, and parents from all over the country bring their children with orthopedic issues for him to treat. And because of his dedication to these children, his clinics are incredibly busy. There's no room to sit or stand or even really walk. Everyone's touching someone else, and babies are laughing and crying and sleeping, feet are being examined, and casts are being cut off. But this special surgeon makes a place for every single person. I watched him as he locked eyes with each child and family member to acknowledge them, and thanked the parents for committing to their children and bringing them back for treatment. He gives every child, whether they're wealthy or poor, a good-natured pat on the cheek and a piece of candy (the poorer kids get the bigger candy bars, because he believes that everyone deserves to be seen and feel worthy). He is incredibly intentional and gentle, and he said to me, looking back over his shoulder as he bent and flexed a small boy's foot, "I have thousands of children. And not to lie, they're a lot of work. But I love them all. I don't need anything else." He's dedicated his entire life to treating these beautifully clubfooted children, and when I asked why in the world he'd voluntarily work six days a week, all hours of the day and many times through the night, he said simply because he has to.

"This is my calling. It's my joy."

And then there's the man who leads all of CURE Clubfoot India. He's also another incredibly humble and giving individual. As a Christian who works in government-run hospitals in the Hindu country of India, he can't verbalize his faith in the same way that the staff in the other CURE hospitals can. But he's a big believer that actions speak louder than words. Even though he can't tell patients and their families about the love of Jesus, he's determined to show them. He firmly believes that every single time he touches a child's foot, he's giving them Jesus. When he smiles at a mother, he is giving them Jesus. He's letting God work through him, and has surrendered *everything* for that work to be done effectively.

He's changing lives, and spreading the love of Jesus. Without having to say anything.

These two men are standing beautiful simply by accepting who God made them to be in the context of the job they were made to do: help the Indian children with clubfeet. But what inspired me most was seeing their faith in action. I was inspired to take a look at my own life; how could I put *my* faith in action? What would that even look like? At school, with my friends? On the street, meeting new people? And then, how could I channel my inner Dr. Matthews? How could I follow his example and love fearlessly? What could that mean for me? For you? For the world?

I had to *live* somewhat fearlessly sooner than I'd thought. I'd been told I was going to speak to 1,400 high schoolers. Which is a lot. So, of course I'd spent a bit of time stressing about it and preparing, and when I showed up on campus I think I laughed out loud. There were paintings on the outside walls of little children playing together, and there were actual little children walking through the front doors into the school. Entire families of four drove by on their motorcycles to drop their children off, and students hopped and skipped in their Disney-themed backpacks.

This was *so* not a high school.

It was monsoon season in India while I was there, which meant that along with being so hot you wanted to fall over and die and so humid that you worry you'll actually fall over and die from sweating so much, it also rained. At random and unexpected times. A *lot* of rain. It started raining right as we walked into what I learned was an elementary school, so of course I showed up dripping wet. (And sweaty. #india)

They took us into a big room with about fifty nine- and ten-year-olds sitting cross-legged on the floor. The moment we walked in, their heads all turned in unison—I swear—like they'd been practicing, and they made prayer hands and bowed their heads—at the same time—and said completely and perfectly together, "Namaste!", which I've learned is not just a cliché word people say at the end of each yoga class but is actually "hello" in Hindi. I awkwardly bowed my head too and said "hello!" in my very out-of-place and suddenly screechy American accent, and then was directed to stand in the front of the room. I smiled and waved probably too eagerly at all the kids seated eerily quiet at my feet, and was given the signal to begin.

Remember that I'd prepared for a mass audience of sixteen-to-eighteen-year-olds—so what I'd planned to say wasn't appropriate for a younger audience. I had to formulate a talk on the fly. Not that it'd be hard (I know the story of my life, of course), but I'd have to make it applicable to these younger Indian kids.

I tried to quickly think up a format for a talk that somehow would make sense to them at their age and still not use too-big words or make my story traumatic in any way.

Oh boy.

"Hello!" (They all said hello in unison back to me, then returned to their quiet and unmoving posture. It was a bit unnerving.)

"My name's Chloe, I'm seventeen years old, and I live all the way across the world in California, which is in the United States. I'm really excited to be here with you guys today to talk about loving ourselves and about what makes us different—and that it's okay to be different!" (The translator did her thing.)

Somehow, I told my story without scarring any child, and when I mentioned the whole "I have a foot deformity" aspect of my life, the kids quickly leaned forward and climbed on each other, trying to get a glance at my foot. I laughed.

I talked about how everyone's different in their own unique way, and that it's *okay*, and how bullying happens in a ton of different forms, and it's a big bummer, but we can change it by first loving ourselves so we can love others.

And of course I talked about standing beautiful—how I want them all to be able to love themselves for the special kids they are. I had them all stand up and do a little happy dance (because I knew it'd be cute) to celebrate themselves for who they are, and then we all shouted, "I Stand Beautiful!" in Hindi, and they loved it. I loved it.

"Main bahut khoobasoorat hoon!"

"I am beautiful!"

It again reminded me of what I think, at this point in my life, my mission is: to help people all over the world love themselves for who they are, let them know that they're special and perfect and that they're no mistake, and invite them to stand beautiful.

But what I've also learned is that it's so much bigger than that. For starters, I was never in control, and never will be. But also, the biggest takeaway was that it's not even "my mission" to get people to stand beautiful; it's God's. Stand Beautiful isn't my thing—it never was. And I saw that even more clearly during the CURE tour. People are starting to love themselves and accept their perfect imperfectness and choose joy and *stand beautiful*, and it's out of my hands. And I love it.

CHAPTER 12

LOOKING *Forward*

I SAW THAT THREE-YEAR-OLD VICTOR WAS already under anesthesia, and they'd uncovered his tiny brown leg and painted it with the orange surgical dye. I stood in the back as the head surgeon selected the appropriate scalpel, sized it out, and made the first cut.

Right on the inside arc of the left clubfoot.

Right where I have a scar.

Where I had close to the same surgery.

When I was also just three years old.

I looked closer. I didn't see the surgeon moving things around in there, exposing the tendons, cutting and slicing and healing. I didn't see the scalpels or the cauterizer or even the anesthesiologist stationed at his post. Instead I saw myself; little three-year-old me on that table. Being cut open. In that same place. And *then* I saw the surgeon moving things around, the scalpels and the cauterizer and even the anesthesiologist stationed at his post. But it was still me on the table.

I know that having this tendon transfer surgery was a very important moment in Victor's life. With time, it will allow his clubfoot to lie straight and flat, and will enable him to walk and skip and run and jump like he should. But it was also a very important moment for me.

In that operating room, watching the surgeon work in the same place my surgeon worked on me, was surreal. And it kind of gave me the chills. I was witnessing what had happened to my body.

I looked down at my scar.

My scar.

And I was proud.

I've always loved my scars because they're a permanent reminder of everything I've gone through, but seeing the actual surgery that gave me the scar made me even more proud of this body. This body that's able to heal. This body that's suffered immense amounts of trauma over and over again. This body that God made me. For me.

And in that room, in the little area of Kijabi on top of the mountain in Kenya, I was reminded of just how beautiful it all is.

Medicine. The opportunities it gives these broken children.

Our bodies. Their ability to heal and start over.

This God. Who enables it all to happen.

And as I saw Victor's new scar be born, and in my

mind's eye saw my own etched scar, I thought about the world and its scars. Because everyone *has* scars. Visible and not, outside or hidden, *everyone* has them as a reminder of where a wound has left its mark. As something signifying a past hardship. As proof we are *stronger.*

I was transported back to late afternoons during my freshman year, sitting at my desk reflecting on hard days and carefully writing *beautiful* over my biggest scar. And that's what it's all about, really. I didn't know it at the time, but it's all about how we choose to see ourselves. The everyday decision to wake up and love the skin we're in, as well as the situations we've been put through. To just simply and truly *love.* Fearlessly. Ourselves, our God, our world. To accept our bodies as the perfectly imperfect canvases and praise proclamations they are. To choose love and joy and peace and be content being fully and unapologetically you. Beautiful.

Which brings me to where I am now. And hopefully where I'll go.

I'm arranged on the table as the artist pulls out everything he needs: the gun and the needles and the ink and all sorts of other stuff. He tests the gun, and the frequency of the monotone buzzing changes as the artist plays with different speeds. He pours antiseptic and antibacterial and anti-everything on my foot and tells me that he's ready to start.

I'm already stinging. And the needle hasn't touched me yet.

It's like this buzzing from deep in my bones suddenly boils up and breaks the surface. Fire erupts and everything is hot. I have no sense of where the needle is on my body or how long it's been since it started. Every curve of the gun rips circles out of my body and digs deep, to the bone. I close my eyes tightly and will myself to think and breathe.

I try to blot out the pain and think about what brought me to this tattoo parlor in Frankfurt, Germany. I recall my earliest memories of pain: The surgery when I was three, waking up wondering where Mom and Dad were. The time when I was ten, and the pain was so intense inside my bones that all I could do was squeeze my eyes shut and hope for a pain-stopping miracle. The brokenness and shame that burned like red-hot fire throughout my heart and mind as I was being assaulted. The next year of pain that was caused by fear and doubt and loneliness and sadness. So. Much. Pain.

But as I'm on that tattoo table, I realize that pain has led me to talk—to share about my pain with others so they wouldn't have to hurt so much. I think about all the amazing joy that has come from that pain—all the smiles, laughter, togetherness. And nothing can ever take that away. I realize that pain and joy actually can and do coexist—because without pain, how can you really know joy? I wouldn't wish all my pain on anyone, anytime, anywhere, but there is beauty in realizing that through pain comes truth and beauty.

Through pain can also come strength and hope and love. And that is good.

The buzzing stops. I'm patted dry and oiled, and I sit up. When I look down toward the end of the table, I see it.

This statement, this challenge, this praise, this permanent, everyday choice, is etched on the outside of my twisted foot. I look down and am reminded forever of the goodness of God and the promises He keeps.

Four consonants. Five vowels.

Nine little cursive letters that change everything. *beautiful.*

People often ask me what standing beautiful *really* means. Which is definitely a good question, because I talk about it a lot. Before the CURE trip, I would say that to stand beautiful means to "embrace your uniqueness and boldly face your beautiful self."™ Which, by the way, is still true. But maybe a little vague and a little hard to understand. Not as in depth as what it truly means for me, now. What it could mean for the world.

Now, I'd have to say that standing beautiful is a mind shift. A choice. We're given only so many days on this earth; and we don't know how many we get, or what they will be like, but we *do* know that each and every day is a gift. And by not loving ourselves, we are missing out on what that gift could mean for us. When we love ourselves, and believe that we were put here, on earth, for a purpose, we can finally do the work God has called us to do. And when we can embrace all parts of ourselves   the back acne that can get worse during the heat, or the fact that thighs may, actually, not have a gap, or that hey, I have a deformed foot—we can move beyond all that and embrace the life that God has planned for us.

We can experience full and complete joy when we say yes to ourselves, to our crazy lives, to our unknown future, and to God. Guadalupe's joy, the joy that Martha had, and the joy that Dr. Matthews shares with each of his patients—we can have that incredible joy too. Because this body is what will help us do the work that God wants us to do.

I'm ready to say yes. And I hope you are too.

Stand beautiful with me. With us.

Join the movement.

ACKNOWLEDGMENTS

*F*irst of all, none of this could have been possible without the One who actually made me. From the very beginning of my life in utero, God has been fully present, fully aware, fully amazing. So thanks, God.

There are so many people who have walked on this journey with me, and for that, I am incredibly thankful.

Dad, since I was born, you have been my constant supporter, my favorite storyteller, my number one brainstormer, and my go-to IT guy. You have never once doubted me, have gone along for my every ride, and have willingly listened to all of my girl drama. Thank you for teaching me to choose joy, and for loving me in the moments it's hard to make that choice. You will forever be my enabler, my encourager, my dreamer, and my fellow gelato lover. I la lu.

Mom, you make everything fun. Thank you for being the ultimate travel buddy, and for teaching me how to be adventurous and brave. Your honesty and authenticity have always inspired and challenged me, and I strive to have your same "if you want it, go get it" attitude. Thank you for being My Person through all the friend drama, the boy problems, my doubts about the future, and my amazement at the bigness and smallness of the world. You make me want to be the best Chloe I can be, and I am forever thankful for our relationship.

Tucker!! You are the best buddy a sister could ever want. I love our adventures, our movie nights, are "which *Office* character am I more like" debates, and our karaoke competition stories. Thank you for making every day full of new surprises, and for teaching me at a very young age about patience and forgiveness (lol). You make me a happier, more positive, livelier, and friendlier person than I ever would have been if not for you. Stoked to keep doing life with you, bud.

Nanny and Papa, with your wild stories, crazy adventures, entertaining voice mails, and never-ending support, you are the *ultimate* grandparents. I love you way more than you will ever know, and it's so fun to share this crazy journey with you. Thank you for always going out of your way to spend time with me. I hope to one day be as adventurous and carefree and confident as you two are, and dream of finding someone who loves me as well as you love each other. Thank you for setting an incredible example of how to live a full life, and I'm excited to see where this journey takes us in the future. Love you both!

Hardt family, I love your support. And Auntie Kimmy— thank you for coming to The Best Day of My Life (#tedtalk)!

Your collective love, laughter, and support are endlessly appreciated. So, so thankful for you guys!!

Marianne, my sister in spirit and love and inside jokes: thanks for sticking around since 2006. You make us, the Howard family, happier and sillier than we might be without you, and we love it when you come hang out and bring your love of dance parties. You've been there for all my biggest moments, and I know you'll be there for the rest of them . . . Thanks for being you. And for making me a better me. LOVE YOU!!!

Margot Starbuck, writer—you created a structure of support and words from which I could jump from and soar. Thank you for your enthusiastic support throughout this journey.

Jacque Alberta, editor extraordinaire, who never tired of my many questions. Thank you for your direction and support throughout this crazy process, for believing in me and my vision, and for giving some incredible advice. Forever thankful (and probably in debt) to you.

Annette Bourland, VP of Publication—you believed in me from the start. Thank you for supporting me and putting your faith in me so early in the process, for listening to my opinion when I didn't know I could have one, and for honoring me and my family and our truth. I owe this entire book opportunity to you—thank you, thank you, thank you.

Londa Alderink, VP of marketing—thank you for

believing in my story, for sharing it with others, and for your incredible and creative ideas. So thankful for you!

Mark Oestreicher (whose buddies call him Marko), you saw something special in me, and have not failed to present me with new and exciting opportunities since. Thank you for believing in me.

Calvary family, thank you for loving me so well through these crazy years. You created a space where I felt loved and appreciated and heard, and I will always remember my time with you.

Wombies ("womb-ies"), you listened every Wednesday night and loved on me when I needed loving, so thank you for hearing me. And especially to Evalyn, Miranda, and Erica; I literally could not have done this without you guys. Endless love for you three.

Andrew West, you have always spoken truth into my life. Thank you for answering my hard questions, for meeting me for coffee so many times, and for being such a key participant in my important decision to get baptized, and for the special day that was. It was so sweet to share that choice with you.

Matt Pohlson, you started a company that changed my life. You were there with us the night I met my hero and have become a true friend. Thank you for supporting me always, enabling me from the start, and for sticking around. I'm so thankful for you and honored to know you!!

Mark Sylvester and Kymberlee Weil, you believed in me from the very beginning and haven't stopped since.

Mark—thank you for taking the time to talk to fifteen-year-old me at that New Year's party, and for introducing me to the idea of giving a TEDx talk. Kymberlee—thank you for helping me find my "hero version," for letting me know it's okay if I cry on stage, and for being the best voice coach I ever could have wanted or asked for. I am forever thankful, appreciative, and *blessed* to know you two, and look forward to many more years of TEDx reunions.

Ann Huntley, DA master—you asked the tough questions and supported me fiercely. So thank you. You were my warrior before I knew I needed one, and you taught me to never doubt my truth. Thank you for believing in me, and for helping me believe in myself.

Dr. Mosca, with your incredible mustache and gentle voice, you taught me that hospitals don't have to be a scary place, and surgeries didn't always have to be a bad thing. You started me on the journey toward healing, and I am forever grateful.

Dr. Diab, who makes me laugh at each visit—thank you for encouraging me to be tough, for answering my endless questions, and for being like a friend in this long process. You literally healed me.

Tracy Curtis, PA, who showed me that women in the orthopedic world can, and do, *rock*!! Thank you for always being so welcoming and friendly, and for representing me during the trial. We love you!

Courtney Sullivan—I may be biased, but you're the best PT in the world. Thank you for always laughing at my bad jokes; massaging my scars, because it just feels *so good*; and for being my buddy for these past eight years. Forever thankful for you and our relationship :)

Mrs. Peters, Mr. Adams, and Mrs. Bonner, thanks for always believing in me, supporting me, and showing me that I was worth more. You've made a difference.

Bono—You've played such a key role in my life since June 10, 2015. Thanks for your words, your engagement, your support, and your availability. You encouraged me to step out of my depression and helped me find purpose and a mission. Thank you, Bono.

Jesus, thanks for loving me so well. I've asked You to show up time and time again, and you *have*. Forever yours, dude.

And to the thousands of people around the world who support me by praying, by following my journey, by allowing me to speak into them, and by speaking into me—thank you.

I stand beautiful with you!!

With love,

Chloe

LESSONS LEARNED

s I prepare to graduate from high school, I've come to realize that who I am today is because of everything I've walked through over the last four years. Some experiences, I never would have chosen: the assault, my surgeries, depression, a legal trial. But I'm also very aware that those very things led to many experiences I never could have dreamed of: meeting Bono, giving a TEDx Talk, traveling around the world with CURE. And because of all this, I've learned some valuable lessons I probably wouldn't have learned if I hadn't been born with a clubfoot, or been assaulted, or battled depression. My hope and prayer is that one of these lessons will resonate with you, and you might discover something about yourself or your own journey.

DIFFERENCES DON'T HAVE TO BE FEARED OR REJECTED.

Our differences make us who we are: unique and beloved children of God. But for some reason, we tend to stick with what we know—and with people who look, talk and act like us. In the end, that can lead to hiding or not fully sharing the part of us that makes us special and unique.

I believe that God designed each of us, on purpose, to be different, and those differences are what make each of us uniquely worth knowing and loving. And when we are true to what makes us unique, we can be recognized, seen, heard, known, and loved for who we truly are.

So when you meet someone who's different than you are, try something new—treat them the same way you would treat anyone else. And open your heart to newness. New experiences, new people, new friendships. Difference is good. Give it a chance.

FORGIVENESS IS HARD, BUT WORTH IT.

Many people think that forgiving someone is easy to do. But in my experience, it's *really* hard. Pain and depression made it hard, those who tried to minimize what happened made it hard, expectations made it hard, *a lot* of things made it hard. But because forgiveness is such an important part of the Christian story, I knew that forgiveness was for me, in my future, at some point. And it should be for you as well. Even if it takes a long time. Even if it takes longer than people think it should. I knew I didn't want to stay stuck in my gross, disgusting, lonely, and bitter world, so even when I didn't want to forgive, I was determined to get there someday.

As you wrestle to forgive those who have hurt you, treat your heart with care. Be gentle with your feelings and with your wounds. If you rush to forgive because you feel pressured, you risk inauthentic forgiveness. But if you wait too long, you risk the hardening of your own heart. It's all about balance, time, and being honest. And remember that no one can tell you when it's the right time to forgive, or force you to do it—that decision is *yours* to make.

If you know it's the right time but are struggling to forgive, like I was, it's important to ask God to aid you in the whole forgiving process. If the wound is still fresh, that request might be as simple as, "God, I don't feel like forgiving. Help me get there eventually." If the wound is a bit older, you might think about praying, "God, I want to be set free. Right now! Help me to forgive. Give me the courage I need."

Once you get there, forgiveness is freeing. And, yeah, there will be days when you might still be a bit mad about what happened, or days when you need to continue to *choose* to forgive, even when you'd rather not. It might take a lot of prayer, time, and energy to finally forgive for good, but the results are worth it.

WHEN WE ADMIT WE'RE BROKEN, WE CAN BE HEALED AND SET FREE.

If I met you, I probably wouldn't be able to read your brokenness immediately in the same way someone would have noticed my huge casted leg as a toddler. But if we hang out for a while, and if you trust me, I bet we'd get to it. You'd share with me the hurt that you carry in your deep places.

And even if I didn't have your experience, I would understand what it means to be broken in that way. If you trusted me with your painful places, I'd respond, "Yeah, me too." And that's where it'd begin. We start by practicing vulnerability with people who are safe. Because when one of us admits, "I'm imperfect; I'm broken; I'm undone; I'm hurting," it makes room for others to do the same.

Taking the brave step to admit you're broken is a way to love yourself and others. All sorts of people will try to convince you that what you've gone through is shameful and that you're alone in what you're going through, that you should just give up. But Jesus confirms that you are worth loving and worth caring for and worth *fighting* for. Begin by offering your deep hurts to God. Let Him heal you and move you and shape you and love you. That's the first step toward redemption. Then, pay attention. There is no end to the number of ways God can show up. It might be through the wise words of others, or through a professional counselor, or through some prayer ministry. It might even be noticing that when you're honest and genuine and real, people *still* love and accept you. Just as you are. Open your heart and your eyes and your mind to see how God will care for you. You might be surprised.

PAIN WILL PASS (EVENTUALLY).

I was so broken inside. I felt used and dirty and shamed and worthless and alone. And when I was deep inside that darkness, it was hard to think the sun would ever shine again, that there could ever be light at the end of the tunnel, that things could get better. But they did. Not only was my season of deep darkness followed by some amazing experiences and opportunities, I now have hope that my future will be bright as well. I know that might not change what you're facing today, but I want you to hear that others who've been overwhelmed by depression and sadness and anxiety and pain have landed on the other side. Have survived.

If you're in the middle of your own darkness, you might not be able to see any light at all. I get that. And that's why it's so important not to isolate yourself. Talk to your parents. Confide in someone from church. Share with a counselor at school. Let them hold you and support you and remind you that you're strong enough to overcome whatever it is you're going through. Take one little tiny baby step, today, tomorrow, next week, next year, *whenever* you're ready, toward getting the help you need. Fight for yourself. You're worth it.

I'M STRONG ENOUGH, AND YOU ARE TOO.

I know this sounds cliché, but before I had to face all the hard feelings my assault stirred up in me, I didn't fully understand or know what I was made of. I'd faced hard obstacles, but I'd gotten through it all and that was that. But in that challenging season after my assault, I began to learn that I'm big enough and strong enough and capable enough to survive brokenness and to thrive. And you are too. God's love for us and plan for our lives is bigger and better than any obstacles we face.

Notice the thoughts that float around in your head throughout the day. That little voice that insists you're weak, you're incapable, you're unworthy? Lies. *All lies.* You can choose to reject those lies. You have the power to do that. You *can* do it. You've got this! God has equipped you with all you need to come out of this and thrive. He'll help you get through it. And He'll never leave you. (Never. Not ever.)

WHEN WE ACCEPT OURSELVES, WE CAN FINALLY ACCEPT OTHERS.

If I don't feel comfortable with parts of myself—my scarred foot, or my skinny chicken leg, or my random acne that decides to show up at the most inconvenient times—then I'm going to have a difficult time accepting others. But when I decide that I'm good enough, exactly the way I am, I'm set free to accept others. And what's really cool about living this way is that it doesn't really depend on what anyone else thinks of you; you can choose, for *yourself*, what your labels are. And you can make the decision to accept others too.

I believe in a God who knows me. He knows that when we don't see ourselves clearly, there's no way we can see others clearly. For me, that means that when I'm cool with the fact I don't have toenails, then I can be cool with other people's differences too. And it's also a reminder that bullies who pick on a little speck of someone else's difference have to take a big old look at their own speck. When they can see themselves clearly, and accept themselves, they'll also be better able to accept others.

Accepting yourself doesn't mean you're going to look in the mirror tomorrow morning and see a supermodel. It means that you can decide to accept yourself *exactly* as you are. It means saying, "Hey, my foot (or nose, or squeaky voice, or whatever) is *good enough*. I'm grateful to be me." And then do the same for others by deciding, "I can accept that girl just the way she is," and "I don't need him to be in any way different than just how he is." After you begin practicing it, you'll find it's a pretty liberating way to live. (And people will *love* being around you. Which is always a plus.)

GOD IS WITH ME. AND GOD IS WITH YOU.

For a long time, I was waiting for God to show up, because I couldn't see Him working in my life. Maybe I was hoping for a fiery talking bush or a deep voice from the clouds. But when I finally looked around, I *could* see signs of God's presence. I looked behind me and saw what God had done in the past. I looked around me and saw God working through others: a hug from my mom, a text from my youth group leader, a call from Tucker on the walk home from school, a call to Papa on the way there, an opportunity to share my story, a sketch from Bono. And then I could look in front of me and know that God would be in my future. When I could recognize God's care for me, my eyes were opened to what God was doing in my life and in others'.

God will always be there for you, even when you can't see Him. He's waiting for you with open arms, whether you choose to run into them or not. In times of confusion and doubt, remember what is most true: God is with you. And God is for you.

MY VOICE MATTERS AND YOUR VOICE MATTERS AND EVERYONE'S VOICE MATTERS.

One of the many good things that has come from my assault is the discovery of my voice. It's easy to dismiss the importance of speaking up for what's right by reasoning, "I'm only a teenager," or "What I have to say doesn't matter." But what you have to say *does* matter. You might not speak to audiences like I do (or maybe you do?), but you have a voice in so many other ways. You might start blogging. Or launch a podcast. Or become a peer counselor. Or encourage a friend who's hurting. Or say that thing during a class discussion that you *know* needs to be said. It doesn't really matter *how* we use our voices—it only matters that we *do*.

Take notice of what you're passionate about, and say yes to the opportunities you have to use your voice for what matters most.

GOD CREATED YOU WITH A PURPOSE.

For years, my mom told me that I'd been created for a purpose, but I didn't really understand what that meant. It just sounded nice, you know? The things your mom tells you because she can. And in the Bible, God uses words like that too. But those words felt like they were meant for some chosen prophet like Esther from the Old Testament, not for a sixteen-year-old girl in California.

Esther's story always seemed so heroic. She was a Jewish girl who was chosen to become queen of Persia around the time all the Jews there were placed in danger. Her cousin Mordecai, who'd adopted and raised her, challenged Esther to live out the unique purpose for which she'd been created, saying, "For if you remain silent at this time, relief and deliverance for the Jews will arise from another place, but you and your father's family will perish. And who knows but that you have come to your royal position for such a time as this?" (Esther 4:14). He was saying, "You were created *for this moment*, given *this* role in the kingdom, so you could use your voice to benefit others." Esther, bold and courageous, was willing to step up and do what she could (#goesther, #yougogirl).

Like my mom's words, I realized God's words in the Bible don't just sound nice: they're real, and they apply to us today as well, even if we aren't queens in Persia. We've all been created for a reason, to make a difference in our lifetimes.

I don't know the unique purpose for which God has designed you. But because of what I've seen God do in my life, I'm confident that if you make yourself available, if you stand with an open posture and say, "I'm available for work!", God will show you the work He's designed you to do. All God needs is your availability.

IF YOU'RE BEING BULLIED

REMEMBER, BULLYING ISN'T ALWAYS EASY TO SEE.

Quite a few people assume that bullying only means getting beat up on the playground at recess or thrown into a trash can in the school cafeteria. But bullying comes in all sorts of forms. It can be physical, verbal, and emotional. It can happen face-to-face and it can happen on your phone. Bullying can be obvious and it can be the hardest thing to see. And that's why bullying is so dangerous.

KNOW YOU ARE *NOT* ALONE.

There are others going through bullying too. Even if you sometimes feel like you're entirely alone, that no one knows or understands the pain you're suffering, remind yourself that those statements are *lies*. There are people who *want* to hear your truth and your pain. There are people who *want* to support you. *Let them.* If you don't know who those people are, ask God to show you. Because He will.

TAKE CARE OF YOURSELF.

While I was being assaulted, I didn't know I could fight back and stand up for myself. I didn't know I was allowed to, or that I had the power or authority to do so. Now, I know that I'm worth protecting and loving and fighting for—and the same is true of you. So if you're being violated, don't be afraid to yell and wrestle and scream and fight. If you've been violated, give yourself time and space to heal. And then, gather the courage you need to face the difficulty of what you're going through; ignoring your feelings only allows them to fester. *You're worth it.* The way past your pain is to plow through it; your long-term self-esteem and healing are worth the struggle.

TELL AN ADULT.

Pain thrives in the darkness. But when you choose to break the silence, you outwit all that pain and brokenness and evil. The reason so many people kill themselves every year is because they've bought into the lie that they're *alone* in their suffering. And I get that, because I felt like that. Sometimes, I still do. But when God gave me the courage to talk about the hurt in my heart, I found that there were people waiting to listen. Waiting to confirm that I was not alone. So tell an adult you trust about what you're going through, and don't be afraid to do it again whenever you feel old doubts starting to surface. Get that affirmation. You're not alone. You never were.

REFUSE TO HARM YOURSELF.

When I was in the deepest, darkest moment of my depression and shame and guilt—the very center of that very bad place—I was home alone one day, cutting an apple. I remember looking at the knife I was using and having the thought that I could, theoretically, end my life. It wasn't a thought I planned to execute, but I knew it was possible. I could see myself theoretically turning that little knife around and jamming it right into my stomach below my ribs. I could see myself theoretically pulling it out, placing it on the counter, then falling to the ground and just lying there, all peaceful, feeling only my physical pain, which blinded me from my emotional pain. It was all theoretical, but I could see it. And that scared me.

When my brother and I were young, my mom talked to us about the times that would come, when life would get really hard. And she talked about suicide, saying, "We always have choices, but that's not one of them. Yes, it's a 'choice' you can make, but there aren't any more choices after that one. Death is forever." I remembered her words in that moment, and chose to place my apple slices in a bowl with a spoonful of almond butter, wash the knife, and place it back in the knife block. I made the choice.

You can make the choice too. The choice to keep going.

You're worth protecting, even when you don't feel like you are. You're worth so much more than whatever happened to you or how your bully made you feel. If you have thoughts about harming yourself, talk to an adult you trust. Remember that suicide is a very permanent solution to a very temporary problem. Make the choice to keep fighting. You can get through this.

GIVE YOURSELF TIME AND SPACE TO HEAL.

I spent months in therapy and personal reflection in order to come to terms with what had happened to me. And after that, I *still* felt vulnerable and afraid. I needed more time. I feel so fortunate that my parents didn't tell me to suck it up and just *deal*. To get over it. Instead, they gave me the time and space I needed to heal. If you don't have a trustworthy advocate who's walking with you through your own healing journey, that's okay; you can be your own advocate. Carve out the time and space you need to heal; your heart will thank you.

NEVER DOUBT YOUR SELF-WORTH.

After my assault, I felt used, worthless, ashamed, and ugly. I felt bad about myself and my body, and doubted my value. So I get it. We don't always love ourselves, and quite often certain circumstances can make previous insecurities even bigger. But despite all the experiences you will go through and the situations you face, I believe you can choose, every day, to embrace what is most true about you. The truth that you are uniquely beautiful and precious. That you are worth loving and celebrating. I know it's not easy, but I encourage you to cling to your truths. #istandbeautiful.

KNOW THE BULLIES ARE HURTING TOO.

"Hurt people *hurt* people." Perpetrators have usually suffered hurt and challenges of their own. That being said, I know that while we were being bullied, we *really* didn't care that our bullies were maybe suffering too. But in the moment, that wasn't our job to acknowledge. Our only job was to protect ourselves physically and emotionally. But as time passes, it *becomes* our job to acknowledge the other person. It's worth noticing that people who are healthy and whole on the inside don't feel the need to bully others. When you're able, consider your bullies and, apart from your eventual forgiveness, make a point to think about their personal situations. You don't suddenly have to have a ton of sympathy for those who bullied you or even interact with them (if you're not in the emotional space to), but just take a moment to recognize their past and their future and who's hurt them. It will change how you see them as an individual, and might even help you better deal with that person in the future.

Consider others; that's what standing beautiful is, in an essence.

Expect life to get better.

When I say "life will get better," I'm not dismissing what you might be facing right now. Just the opposite. I know exactly how life-altering and fun-ruining pain and grief can be in the aftermath of bullying. I get it. But I also believe that you and I are still gaining life skills to help us cope with everything we're facing. And sometimes we gain those skills the hard way. I want you to hear that the pain you're feeling right now will pass. It *will* get better.

THREE ACTION POINTS OF

STANDING BEAUTIFUL

ONE: WE'RE EMBRACING OUR UNDENIABLE
WORTH AND BEAUTY.

Because God made you YOU, you're completely and undeniably worthy. Fully, one hundred percent worth it. Your inherent dignity and value are irreplaceable. *No one* can steal it from you. Nothing anyone can say about you or do to you can change the fact that you are precious and beloved and *worth* love and respect. When you stand beautiful and accept yourself as you are, you choose to agree with what God has deemed is most true about you. And that's pretty cool.

TWO: WE'RE REDEFINING "NORMAL."

I think it's time to redefine normal. Some people say I don't look "normal," but the way my deformed foot looks is normal to me. It's my reality. And because we all have different realities, "normal" doesn't actually exist. Maybe you have parents that fight. Maybe you have a different skin color than the majority, or maybe you don't own the right clothes. Maybe you're "too short" or "too tall" or "too plain." Or maybe you're not the best writer, or you struggle with math, or you really can't remember anything about the War of 1812. We're *all* different; good at some things, not great at others; have parts of us that are unlike anyone else; or have beliefs that someone else might not share. And it's okay for us to all be unique in our looks, our likes and dislikes, and in our personal choices. So why put so much time and effort into making ourselves into the cookie-cutter standard of "normal" when we are perfect in our own unique ways?

All sorts of people will try to tell you that you need to be someone other than who you are. And sometimes your own voice will try to tell you that. It badgers you to "fit" the world's standard of what is "normal," what is "acceptable," what is "beautiful." But the truth is you are acceptable as-is, and beauty can't be squeezed into a mold. Let's look at the world differently. Let's be different. And make it okay.

THREE: WE'RE REFLECTING THE BEAUTY OF OTHERS.

To stand beautiful is to accept yourself exactly as you are. And when we *do* accept ourselves as we are—when we choose to stop freaking out about our weight, our hair, our skin, our clothes, our social status, etc.—we can accept *others* exactly as they are. Even if you don't look in the mirror and break into a spontaneous dance of joy, as you practice standing beautiful—accepting yourself and accepting others—you dive right into what is most true about you. What is most true about others.

It feels good to be around someone who thinks you're absolutely amazing. Your grandmother, your friend, your teacher. Your papa, who you can call every morning on the way to school to complain about boys. You like to be around these people because they see you as someone who's amazing and beautiful and worthy of their time and respect. But you can also make the choice to *be* that person for someone else—like listening to your papa when he complains to you about his aging body, and telling HIM he's still amazing and wonderful, no matter what. There's no age requirement, no application, no community service hours needed. When you're content with who you are, you can show that they're accepted and beautiful and unique and amazing and worth it too.

INTERVIEW WITH CHLOE HOWARD

Want to know more about Chloe? Here are some frequently asked questions that give the inside scoop!

Q: Chloe, do you have your driver's license, and if you do, what kind of car do you drive?

A: I got my license a few months after I turned sixteen. And the car I drive is pretty incredible. She *turns heads*. Her name is Bertha, and she's a 2004 dark blue Honda Odyssey minivan. Her chipped, dented, and rusting paint job is noticeably sparkly (I don't really know why), and she has blue flames on both sides. She's fantastic. (#loml)

Q: What are a few of the books on your bookshelf?

A: I have *a lot* of books. (I love to read!!) Some of my favorites, but not limited to, are:

- *Heaven is for Real*

- *Small Acts of Amazing Courage*
- *Chains*
- *Quiet Power, Teen Version* (obviously)
- *The Book Thief*
- *Girl in the Blue Coat*
- My Bible
- All my journals, which I love to re-read

Q: Do you have pets?

A: Yeah. My family has two dogs. Heather, who's eleven years old, is a gentle and quiet golden retriever. She's got arthritis in her back two legs, and has been proven to be the sweetest dog ever. Charlie, a crazy puppy, is a big Bernese mountain dog. He's sneezy, and slobbery, and playful, and huge. We love them both very much!!

Q: What's on your favorite iTunes playlist?

A: My favorite playlist is about five hours long, and has eighty-one of the VERY BEST songs on it!! It's pretty random, but a lot of it falls into the following categories:

- U2 (of course)
- Christian music by Switchfoot, TobyMac, Hillsong, Matthew West, Francesca Battistelli, Lauren Daigle, and others
- Eighties music
- Nineties music
- Bruno Mars

- "Easy" country music like Rascal Flatts, Hunter Hayes, and Thomas Rhett
- Various pop songs from the Top 40 that I heard on Bertha's janky radio and really liked

Q: What's your favorite Bible verse?

A: My favorite verse is Jeremiah 1:5, which says, "Before I formed you in the womb I knew you, before you were born I set you apart; I appointed you as a prophet to the nations." But I also really, really like Acts 26:16, which says, "Now get up and stand on your feet. I have appeared to you to appoint you as a servant and as a witness of what you have seen and will see in me."

Q: Chloe, how has what you've faced changed you?

A: I'd say I'm more authentic now. When we hide our pain, we have to put on a mask to convince others that everything is okay and we've got it all together. But when we gather courage to face what's inside, it sets us free to be more authentic, accepting both our strengths and our insecurities and weaknesses. And those are the kind of people I'm looking to be friends with—authentic people. I just don't have time for fake people! Life's too short for surface-level relationships. I want to be friends with those who are honest, genuine, real, authentic (and a little wacky).

About The Author

CHLOE HOWARD IS ON A mission to empower people of all ages to embrace their uniqueness and boldly face their beautiful selves. Born with a foot deformity, Chloe had five major operations by the time she was fifteen. Through her hardships, Chloe learned that differences are unique, bullying needs to be stopped from the inside out, and worth is most valuable when it comes from within. Today, Chloe is the voice of Stand Beautiful, a movement promoting the acceptance of self and others. She has been featured on NPR, *Teen Vogue*, and was recently a TEDx speaker. She has been the subject of two documentaries and toured internationally with CURE.org. Visit standbeautiful.me for more information about Chloe and her message.